THE FRAGILE CHAMPION

DORIS BROWN WHO ALWAYS RAN THE EXTRA MILE

Ken Foreman
US Olympic Coach

TATE PUBLISHING, LLC

Published in the United States of America
by Tate Publishing, LLC
127 East Trade Center Terrace
Mustang, OK 73064
(888) 361–9473

This book is designed to provide accurate and authoritative information with regard to the subject matter covered. This information is given with the understanding that neither the author nor Tate Publishing, LLC is engaged in rendering legal, professional advice. Since the details of your situation are fact dependent, you should additionally seek the services of a competent professional.

ISBN: 1–5988611–9–0

DEDICATION

To the ladies of the Falcon Track Club

TABLE OF CONTENTS

PREFACE

This is my view of the running career of Doris Brown. I was her coach from 1960 until 1974 and her colleague from 1975 until 1998. Others have written, often with eloquence, about the performance record of this legend of the track and cross-country trail. Most of what they have written is accurate, but some is not. I hope to set the record straight.

There is another reason for telling my side of this important story. It is because what Doris accomplished—at a time when it was deemed both inappropriate and potentially harmful for females to (1) work against resistance, (2) to move heavy objects, and (3) to sweat profusely—has relevance for runners today. Her best marks of 2:02.2 for 800 meters and 4:14.6 for 1500 meters were made at a time when female athletes did not have appropriate equipment, did not have locker rooms or athletic training facilities, and frequently were not welcome on the track. Such an accomplishment surely attests to the fact that the human will has more to do with success, than equipment, facilities, and competitive opportunities.

In the early days of our relationship, Doris and I searched for answers to questions regarding a females' trainability. More specifically, we wanted to know how often Doris should train, how much should she do, how long should she rest between work segments, how intense ought a training session be, etc. One afternoon, following a training session that proved to be too easy, I was apologizing "for not asking enough." Doris surprised me saying, "It is okay, Coach. I always run an extra mile, anyway." Running the extra mile was a defining characteristic of Doris Brown's amazing running career.

I take full responsibility for the accuracy of what I have

written, having depended upon memory, lengthy discussions with Doris, press reports, articles appearing in the now defunct "Women's Track and Field World," and my personal records. The latter is a detailed account of daily training sessions, as well as summary statements about most of the track and cross-country meets in which Doris participated during her active running career.

INTRODUCTION

More than 40 years ago, I looked up from my desk at Seattle Pacific University and observed a petite, young woman jogging along the sidewalk. What caught my attention were her legs, tightly wrapped from ankle to knee. *Who is this and why the wraps?* I wondered. *What has she done to injure herself?* She crossed the street and started running up Queen Anne Hill. It was perhaps a week later, when I answered a knock on my office door, that I met the bandaged runner. She was a college freshman. Her name was Doris Severtsen. She had come to talk with me about her running.

Doris arrived at Seattle Pacific in the fall of 1960. I had taken time off to complete my dissertation, thus was not actively coaching during the autumn quarter. Doris had heard, however, that I had experience working with female athletes and wondered if I would help her achieve her dream of being a successful runner.

Although we talked only briefly, it soon became apparent to me that this was no idle chatter. This young lady wanted to be, and intended to be, a really successful runner. I told her that I would think about it and set a time when we could have a more extended conversation, wishing her well with her daily run. That was the beginning of a relationship that has lasted until this day.

In the weeks and years that followed, the petite, young lady, with a great burn to succeed, made a coach of me. While setting national and world records, she taught me vastly more than I ever taught her. She taught me about effort and commitment and discipline and the unlimited strength of the human will. She proved my professional training wrong—teaching me that girls and women can train just as hard as boys and men. She showed me that an indomitable spirit would bridge the gap between desire and fulfillment. In short, Doris proved that big dreams and heady expectations are achievable, when and if you are willing to run the long and lonely extra mile.

During her running career, Doris set records at 330 yards, 880 yards, 800 meters, 1500 meters, the mile, 3000 meters, and 2 miles. She was five times the National and five times the World Champion in cross-country. She participated on numerous US International teams, including the 1967 and 1969 Pan American teams and the Olympic teams of 1968 and 1972. Doris was honored by the Washington State Legislature in a proclamation extolling her contribution to the youth of the state. She was selected as the 1971 Seattle "Man of the Year in sports." She is a member of the Track and Field Hall of Fame, the Distance Runners Hall of Fame, the USTF Coaches Hall of Fame, and a charter member of the Seattle Pacific University "Legends Hall of Fame."

Her best times, set more than 40 years ago, would likely place her in the finals of most national championship events contested today. These are 2:02.2/800m, 4:14.5/1500m, 4:39.6/mile, 9:44.6/3000m, 10:07/2 miles. While relative, her best cross-country marks are 1.5 miles/7:14.5, 2 miles/14:28 and 3100m/11:08.4. As impressive as are her accomplishments, the fact that she did any of this and the manner in which she did it, is even more impressive. A high school girl running alone on isolated beaches surrounding Puget Sound, with no encouragement from home, with no female stars to emulate, and with no place to compete—she still wanted to be a runner and would not let it go.

In 1959, Doris heard about a track and field team for girls. She met with the coach, a Mr. McQuarrie, who invited her to join the Mic Macs. Mr. McQuarrie, who had no professional training, provided his girls with opportunities to compete. Doris soon became his star athlete, excelling at both the jumps and running events. By 1960, she was good enough to qualify for the Olympic Trials in the 880y. She placed third at the trials, but did not meet the Olympic qualifying standard. Following the trials and an abbreviated training camp where she moved from 3rd to 2nd in the hierarchy of American women middle distance runners, Doris returned home and prepared to enter Seattle Pacific University. I first saw her running along the sidewalk one month later.

Sitting here now, it is difficult to imagine having one of the top-ranked middle distance runners in America on campus and not knowing who she was or what she had done. Nevertheless, that was the tenor of the times in which we lived. I was an experienced coach, had coached a two-time national champion in the 880y run as well as a nationally ranked female sprinter, but did not know that female athletes were permitted to run races longer than 220y. The fact is that I did not know anyone in the coaching profession who knew or cared that girls and women were capable of running half a mile.

Even now, I am embarrassed to say that it was months before I became fully aware that Doris Severtsen had competed in the 1960 Olympic Trials. She never talked about herself; she came to the track, completed her workout, and returned to her campus job. At some point the light came on for me as I watched Doris train, realizing that she was doing far more than most of the university men with whom I worked. Her commitment to excellence was palpable. I began to realize, too, she was doing all of this in spite of the formidable burden that she carried, a full load of college course work, plus the need to work long hours to pay for room, board, and tuition. With the passing of time, I also became aware that Doris carried a punishing emotional burden, seldom articulated, yet ever lurking among the shadows of her mind.

Doris left the 1960 Olympic training camp with seriously incapacitating shin splints. While these bothered her all of her running career, she was able to run through the pain. However, this was not so when she accrued stress fractures in both feet, when she sustained a serious injury to her hamstring, and when she ruptured the tendon of the peroneus longus muscle during the 1972 Olympic Games. I grimace now when I think of this great athlete working through her pain—physical and emotional—with precious little help from anyone other than teammates and close personal friends. As the record will show, Doris Brown (Heritage) accomplished what she accomplished largely by the strength of her will. I am convinced that she could have done even more in another time, perhaps another place. I believe she, like so many girls and women in those early days, would have benefited from support and assistance from the self-serving hierarchy of the AAU.

The '50s and '60s were difficult times for females who wanted to compete in the athletic domain and for coaches who dared to associate with girls and women who chose to do so. Doris was viewed as an aberration, definitely weird because she chose to run. It was not uncommon for motorists to honk and gesture as they passed her while running on the road. She was not permitted to run on her high school track, and she wore track shoes, shorts, and warm-ups fashioned for boys and men. Many colleges and universities did not even have locker rooms for female students, and a training room was out-of-bounds for women. During the early '60s, I had to take Doris into a closet to massage her injured leg.

As strange as it may seem in this day and age, few physicians understood or cared about the female athlete. I was awakened one night with a knock on my hotel room door when two members of the US Women's International Cross-Country team came to talk. One was crying. In time, she said to me, "I understand you know something about girls not having periods." Between sobs, she managed to tell me that she had visited the health center at UCLA to get advice about her menstrual cycle. "The doctor examined me," she said, and when finished, he looked at me and said, "I'm not sure what to tell you, except that you appear to be half a man anyway.' " So help me God, a young lady on our team competing in Milan, Italy, told me this tragic story.

Not only were female runners harassed, men who dared work with girls and women were harassed as well. Ed Temple, likely the most widely respected women's coach in the world, and I, were sent by our respective state legislatures as official representatives to the First National Conference on Women in Sport. During the opening session, we were singled out by the keynote speaker as "undesirables" and told to go home.

Campus police placed me under arrest on two occasions at the University of Washington for working with female athletes on university facilities. The arresting officer apologized to Doris and me, but stated he was following the orders of a former coach who does not like girls. Virginia Husted, a public school teacher and member of our track and field club, asked me to assist her in conducting an invitational track and field meet for high school girls. We rented the field at Seattle's Nathan Hale High School, and upon arriving to prepare the facility for competition, we were confronted by the boys' high school coach. "Just leave," he said, then spread-eagled himself across the equipment room door. An administrator later informed Virginia that she could lose her job if we continued to force the issue where the girls meet was concerned.

Perhaps the toughest challenge for me was having fellow coaches in the NAIA and NCAA look at me with pity because I was wasting my time on girls. In an ironic twist, several of the most obnoxious debunkers of female athletes later became big names in women's athletics.

In preparing this manuscript, I have attempted to highlight what I know and have experienced regarding the life and times of a great, American, female runner. Chapter 1 describes the "Heartbreak and Tragedy" surrounding a 12-year running career; it helps to place in context the highs and the lows of a life committed to excellence. Chapters 2 and 3 have been written to help the reader see more clearly the so-called human side of athlete and coach. Chapters 4–12 describe the journey—achievements and disappointments—from Doris' first world record set in the Agrodome, in Vancouver, BC, on the night of February 19, 1966, to her first loss of a cross country race, to Francie Larrieu, in November of 1972. I personally think of the material covered here as a tale of uncommon commitment, discipline, injury, rehabilitation, and of great victory and crushing defeat.

Chapters 13–14 are in one sense the ramblings of a coach who has spent 57 years in the trenches. I write about "footsteps" and "night-sounds," the potentially debilitating psycho-factors at loose in the athletes' domain. There also were many so-called peaks and valleys along the way. These are explored in some detail.

The final chapter likely has particular relevance to persons who seek to flee from the clutches of mediocrity, to become the best that they can be. In this chapter, I look back across the years, attempting to account for one girls' journey from tide flats to the top of the athletes' world. It is my sincere hope that some who read the story of Doris Brown will be motivated to move beyond the ordinary.

Finally, rather than burden the manuscript with extensive quotes, schedules, and tables, I have placed these in the appendix. The interested reader, coach, and athlete will find a rich resource among these pages.

HEARTBREAK AND TRAGEDY

BROWN, D. USA N.A. I was stunned! Not more than thirty minutes had passed since Doris and I hugged on the Olympic warm-up track, and now the scoreboard flashed the dreaded initials N. A. What had happened? Why was the scoreboard reporting nonappearance for Doris Brown?

Nearly blinded by tears, I ran out of the stadium, across the highway separating the stadium from the Olympic village, and through a labyrinth of buildings to the warm-up track. She was not there. Someone, I know not who, informed me that a US athlete had been "carried away on a stretcher."

My credentials provided limited access to the Olympic site—the courtyard (where athletes, personal coaches, and family members could meet), the weight room, and a variety of training sites. I did not have access to the housing complex, dining room, or medical facilities. No matter how strong my pleas, I was essentially outside looking in. I ran along the village fence searching for someone whom I knew, anyone who could help me find out what had happened to my athlete. Hours passed, it became an exercise in futility to wait any longer. Frustrated, discouraged, I decided to return to my host home in the village of Ottobrunn. If Doris were attempting to contact me, she would surely leave a message there.

Turning toward the subway station, I noted men in warm-up suits standing on top of one wing of the athletes housing complex. The thought occurred to me that boys will be boys, even at the Olympic Games.

The train leaving the main Olympic Station was crowded; loud talking, laughter, and the press of people added to my emotional pain. As we moved outward from the City Center, the crowd thinned out; only a few passengers remained when the train stopped at Ottobrunn. When we emerged onto the station platform, my senses told me that something was not right. People were standing—mute—as if they were victims of profound tragedy; there was an aura of unexplained pain. I do not speak German, so I walked on not knowing. Then I saw him, my host, former fighter pilot Herman Von Massow, waiting for me on his front porch. Herman was crying. He took me in his arms, and sobbing, he said, "We have tried so hard to make these Olympics a celebration for the world, to show them that we Germans are good people and now terrorists have destroyed all that we have attempted to do."

It was there, on the porch of a German officer's home, I learned that the men whom I had observed on the roof of the dormitory were not boys at play, but were soldiers attempting to capture Arab terrorists who had killed or captured every member of the Israeli Olympic Team.

It is difficult even now to describe the long hours of the night of September 5/6, 1972. I recall that Doris called from the Ottobrunn Station asking for a ride. I remember Brita Von Massow volunteering to drive, and when we arrived, we found a fragile champion standing alone on the platform—crutches and cast, heartbreak within a tragedy, and pain heaped upon profound pain. Britta, Doris, and I returned to the Von Massow residence, where we watched in stunned silence as the "Munich Massacre" unfolded.

Mitchell Bard described those agonizing hours this way:

> "It was 4:30 in the morning of Sept. 5, 1972, when five Arab terrorists wearing track sweat suits climbed the six-foot fence surrounding the Olympic Village. Although they

Ken Foreman

were seen by several people, no one thought anything was unusual since athletes routinely hopped the fence, moreover, the terrorists weapons were hidden in athletic bags. These five were met by three more men who are presumed to have obtained credentials to enter the village.

Just before 5, the Arabs knocked on the door of Israeli wrestling coach, Moshe Weinberg. When Weinberg opened the door he realized something was wrong and shouted a warning to his comrades. He and weightlifter Joseph Romano attempted to block the door while other Israelis escaped, but were killed by terrorists. The Arabs then succeeded in rounding up nine Israelis to hold as hostages.

At 9:30, the terrorists announced that they were Palestinians and demanded that Israel release 200 Arab prisoners and that the terrorists be given safe passage out of Germany.

After hours of tense negotiations, the Palestinians, who it was later learned belonged to a PLO faction called Black September, agreed to a plan whereby they were to be taken by helicopter to the NATO air base at Firstenfeldbruck where they would be given an airplane to fly them and their hostages to Cairo. The Israelis were then taken by bus to the helicopters and flown to the airfield. In the course of the transfer, the Germans discovered that there were eight terrorists instead of the five they expected and realized that they had not assigned enough marksmen to carry out the plan to kill the terrorists at the airport.

After the helicopters landed at the air base around 10:30 pm the German sharpshooters attempted to kill the terrorists and a bloody firefight ensued. At 11, the media was mistakenly informed that the hostages had been saved and the news was announced to a relieved Israeli public. Almost an hour later, however, new fighting broke out and one of the helicopters holding the Israelis was blown up by a terrorist grenade. The remaining hostages in the second helicopter were shot to death by one of the surviving terrorists."[1]

I was a 10-year-old kid, too poor to purchase tickets, when my father took me by streetcar to the Los Angeles Coliseum. There, at the 1932 Olympics, we stood outside . . ."just to hear the cheering . . . a way," my father said . . ."to learn something about discipline and achievement." It is fair to say that the experience in 1932 sensitized me for the length of my life to the challenge and the magnificence of the Olympic Games. It did not prepare me, however, for the heartbreak of having 12 years of work by athlete and coach destroyed in a moment of time. Nor did it prepare me for the black cloud of tragedy that beset the Israeli Olympic team in what has come to be called the "Munich Massacre."

Farms and miles and miles of wooded areas surrounded the village of Ottobrunn. I could sit no longer I needed space and time to put my personal heartache and the overriding national tragedy into perspective. It was the dawn of a new day when I slipped outside, first walking through quiet streets, then vast fields of corn, and finally running off into the woods. I ran and ran and ran—sometimes stopping to sit and think—and then to run again. When I finally returned to the Von Mossow residence, Doris had returned to the Olympic village where she was advised by a German physician to stay on her crutches and see her team doctor as soon as she arrived back in Seattle. We did not know it then, but time and circumstances had taken their toll. Doris was nearing the end of a brilliant running career.

That same day, Avery Brundage, President of the IOC, issued the controversial proclamation that "the games must go on." Competition was delayed for 24 hours, during which 80,000 people attended a memorial service to honor 11 brave men. I did not see Doris again until she arrived home in Seattle, though I did visit the Olympic Stadium one last time.

Very early the following morning, I entered the stadium with the maintenance crew and walked to a place near the victory stand, so small, so alone. With one eye, I looked toward the athletes village where 1000s of athletes—one being my Doris—were preparing for a new day. With my other eye, I looked across half a universe to a strip of sand on the shore of Gig Harbor, Washington. I could almost see her there—this slip of a junior high school girl—hair blowing, arms pumping, and running into the rising sun—an ordinary girl who caught a dream and would not let it go. This is her story, a story of work and struggle, victory and defeat, and a sort of celebration of the strength of the human spirit. I will do my best to tell it as we lived it from our first encounter in 1960 to the heartbreak and tragedy of 1972. Most of all, I want this to be a celebration of the competitive life of a great runner and a way of thanking her for having had the privilege of jogging alongside.

TIDE FLATS AND SAND BANKS

Doris was born and raised in a rural, wooded area near Tacoma, Washington. The family property meandered along side the tide flats of Puget Sound. Doris remembers her early years as mostly happy. She had early morning chores, feeding chickens and tidying up the yard. When there was time, she took great delight in jogging on the rocky beach in search of agates. She paused while telling me about her youth, then said, "I have always enjoyed the early morning; that is likely why it has been so easy for me to start my day by running."

She was clear about her personal faith, but remembered a somber, a sometimes depressive piety at home. Her father was "very controlling," and she said it was her mother who nurtured her dreams and quietly supported her choosing to run. Doris recalled that she "always enjoyed P.E., especially play days where all the kids competed together." She acknowledged, "My younger sister was far more talented than I, but she did not enjoy competition. I did, but was too small to be very successful."

One day while running on the tide flats, Doris had a sense of joy so profound that it was difficult to describe. "Perhaps," she said, "this gave me something of my very own, and I began to recognize that there is great satisfaction in doing our best." It also was about that time when a "situation eventuated" that had a traumatizing effect in her life to this day. I have often wondered what part this personal trauma had in driving her from the tide flats to the top of the runners' world.

Doris attended Peninsula High School in Purdy Washington. She frequently ran to school from her home in Gig Harbor. She was not, however, permitted to run on the Peninsula High School track, nor were there other athletic programs at the high school for girls. For some strange reason, she recalled, she was permitted to run on the track at South Kitsap High School, and occasionally her mother would make the drive to Port Orchard, sitting in the car while Doris ran. In the summer of her sophomore year, Doris was befriended by the Peninsula recreation director who accompanied several kids to a Junior Olympic track and field meet in Tacoma. While there is no record of how well Doris performed, Mrs. Severtsen (Doris' mother) was quoted, saying her daughter was "spotted by Mr. McQuarrie [coach of the Mic Macs] and Mc Quarrie asked her to be on his team."[2]

Doris joined the Mic Mac Track and Field Club—a club for girls, which was organized by an elderly man, whose name was Robert McQuarrie. Initially, Doris wanted to be a jumper, an active interest that she nurtured until problems with her feet forced her to focus on running. She soon was the outstanding performer on the Mic Mac team, running the 220y, 880y, the relays, and when possible, participating in the long jump and high jump.

In 1960, Doris qualified for the Olympic Trials to be held in Abilene, Texas. As was true during most of her competitive career, she and her teammates expended almost as much energy raising travel funds as they did in training. A strong performance at the Far Western AAU meet on June 3 (1st in 880y/2:21.2) caught the attention of the Peninsula Boosters; however, and a "Doris Severtsen Olympic Fund" and a "Dimes for Doris fund" were formed to help with expenses for such a trip, which were assumed to be approximately $200.00.[3] Doris and her Mic Mac teammates departed by train on June 30 for Denver and Corpus Christi, where they participated in so-called "preliminary national try outs" on July 4, 8, and 9. Doris set a National AAU meet record for the 800m (2:20.1) in the prelims but failed to finish in the finals. The following week, Doris won her Olympic trials qualifying heat in 2:20.4, and on July 15, she placed third (2:17.6) behind Pat Winslow (Pat Connolly) and Rose Lovelace in the 880y run.

All three runners went to the pre-Olympics training camp, which was held at Emporia State University. The purpose of the camp was to provide an opportunity for athletes with non-qualifying marks to meet the Olympic Standard (2:12.0). Although Doris improved her 880y time to 2:15.3 and was ranked 2nd in her event, she failed to meet the standard and returned home. The flight from Kansas to Seattle was her first time in the air and would be the first of many flights to compete in track and cross-country meets around the world.

I first saw Doris in the autumn of 1960, outside my office window at Seattle Pacific University. Legs tightly bandaged to alleviate the pain of shin splints, this wisp of a girl—flaxen hair flailing—ran by the gym on her way up the hill to the college cinder track. Working to complete my doctoral dissertation, and on leave from all coaching, I tucked the scene away to be considered another day. That day arrived sooner than expected when Doris came to my office to ask for help. As she shared her goals and expectations, it became obvious to me that we were not engaged in idle chatter. This young lady wanted to be and expected to be an outstanding runner.

I agreed to assist her as much as possible until my writing project was completed, suggesting that we would then decide on how best we could work together. For the next two years, Doris frequently trained with men from the college track and field team. In addition to my verbal input, she was assisted on the track by the interim track coach. During a recent conversation, Doris recalled that her favorite workout those days was to "run hard the 600 meters up hill to the college track, stretch and then run repeat sprints up the steep sand bank that surrounded the field." She noted that she ran these in a series of "5 x 50y or 5 x 75y without rest." As she was reminiscing about her sand bank sprints, I shared a conversation that I once had with Pakka Vasala, 1972 Olympic champion in the 1500m event.

In 1979, Bernie Wagner, Stan Huntsman, Russ Rogers, and I were in Europe for the purpose of finding a training site for the 1980 Olympic Team. While visiting Varamaki, national training center for Finish athletes, I chatted with Pakka Vasala about his epic victory over Kipchoge Keino in the 1972 Olympics. He laughed and said that he attributed his victory to . . ."daily briefings about the awesome work-outs that your Wohluter was doing . . . and about the intense work loads of the Kenyan runners. Hearing such things," he said, "drove me to my sand bank . . . where I worked and worked until I was blinded by sweat. It was that sand bank that earned me my victory at Munich."

My dissertation complete, doctorate in hand, I returned to full-time coaching in the spring of 1962. Doris, and now additional members of a rejuvenated Falcon Track Club, trained daily along side my university men. It soon became obvious that Doris was a diamond in the rough. She was hungry for information about running, a fully committed and tenacious trainer. Not then, or during all of the years that we worked together, did Doris raise questions about a proposed workout. She never asked how much or what was next; she used her energy to get the job done.

Indeed, Doris was so tough on herself that I often was caught up in a dilemma: Let her go or advise her to back off. She and I were plowing new ground, working in an area where there were few precedents to follow. As I struggled with the dilemma of my professional training regarding the "fragile female" and the reality of what I observed Doris do every day, I vacillated between asking too much and too little. The search for balance likely contributed to what Vince Reel once described as "the plague of injures" that were to affect Doris' performance during her college career. She made gains, ran some strong races, but did not reach her potential until 1966. By then, both she and I were more mature in our understanding of the training process and of what women were capable of doing—but that is getting ahead of the story.

Doris completed her undergraduate studies in the spring of 1964. Within weeks of graduation, she contracted to teach at the junior high school level, and she was back on campus working on a master's degree. Caught up in our own little world, we thought that Doris was ready to accomplish big things on the track. The first challenge would come at the National Championship meet at Hanford, California, to be followed by the Olympic Trials at Randal's Island, NY. On June 20, 1964, one month out of college, Doris was 4th at the Hanford meet, running the 880y in 2:15.1—a personal record, but not fast enough to compete with the likes of Sandra Knott, Leah Ferris, and Carol Mastronarde. Doris did less well at the Olympic Trials, placing 6th with a time little better than she had run at Abilene in 1960.

We were disappointed, but expected things to improve during the forthcoming cross-country season. In our first meet, a dual meet between the Falcon Track Club and the Vancouver Olympic Club, Doris ran well enough to win, beating Canada's Thelma Flynn, but was obviously very tired at the finish line. Never one to complain, Doris caught my attention during a postmortem discussion when she revealed she was having difficulty sleeping, was having moments of unexplained anxiety, and was having persistent unexplained fatigue. Was this the cause or a consequence of her less-than-strong performance? It was a question I began to ponder.

Because we had high expectations for 1964, perceiving it as a breakout year in both track and cross-country, our

Falcon Track Club joined forces with Seattle Pacific University and the Seattle Parks and Recreation Department to host the National AAU Cross-Country Championships. The meet attracted runners from across the country, with the two strongest teams representing Sacramento (Wills Spikettes) and San Jose (The Cindergals). We expected strong competition, and we expected Doris to win. This was her home course, her domain.

At the "crack" of the starter's pistol, Doris went into the lead, set a strong pace, and appeared to be in position to win. Then with less than .1 mile to go, a rising star, Marie Mulder, passed Doris and was first to the finish line. During the summer circuit, Doris had been badly beaten on the track and now had lost to a 15-year-old girl in cross-country. It was time for serious soul searching, with two questions needing resolution: Was Doris a competitor capable of winning the big meets, or was she someone who trained hard but faltered when it was time to compete? The second, a corollary question had to do with me: Was I qualified to coach a female distance runner who seemed to have potential for becoming an outstanding performer?

A CARPENTER OR A COACH

My intent in writing this book was to recognize the achievements of a pioneer whose dreams and tenacity helped to negate inaccurate assumptions regarding the physical/emotional prowess of girls and women, and who herself became a world renown runner. I had not intended to write much about myself until persons who read the working manuscript urged me to briefly tell my story, assuring me that it would help to put Doris Browns achievements into proper perspective.

I grew up in Los Angeles during the great depression of the 1920s. Our family was typical for our time. My father went to work each day as a carpenter and my mom stayed home to take care of the kids. Dads were assumed to be strong—the breadwinners. Moms, well, they were just moms. They cooked, cleaned, and did not do heavy physical work because, after all, they were women.

When I arrived in high school, the assumed to be differences between boys and girls became more obvious. Boys turned out for athletics—there was no such thing as an athletic program for girls. We also learned that girls had a monthly downtime when we observed them sitting on a bench at the side of their PE field. Girls that I knew did not engage in serious physical activity where as I competed in four sports. In 1936, as a high school freshman, I competed at class C, meaning that I was small for my age. For a reason unknown now, I chose to work with the shot put. My high school training partner in the shot put was to become a renowned ophthalmologist and an Olympic gold medal winner in platform diving. His name was Sammy, better known now as Dr. Sammy Lee. In my senior year, I weighed 160 pounds, was the world record holder in the rope climb, and placed 4th in the shot put in the Los Angeles City Relays. My best put with the 12# shot was about 54'.

After graduating from high school, I went to work full-time as a carpenter, expecting that to be my lifetime work. In the evenings, I frequently trained in gymnastics at the Los Angeles Turnverein. When possible, I entered open gymnastics competition in meets sponsored by the Metropolitan Amateur Athletic Union. Sometime in 1941, while watching a track and field meet at Occidental College, I took an interest in the javelin. Having a strong arm, it seemed to me that this was an event in which I might achieve some success. I purchased two wooden javelins and now divided my training time between the Turnverein and an open field near my home in Highland Park, a suburb near the Rose Bowl in Southern California. My best throw, without any coaching, was about 200'.

Life was good. I was earning a good living, staying sharp as a gymnast, and learning to throw my beloved javelin. Then one fall evening, upon returning home from work, I learned that we were at WAR. Some days later, I attempted to enlist in the Navy, but was rejected because of a torn knee cartilage. Later I enlisted in the Coast Guard and was shipped to the training base at Government Island, in Alameda, CA. While there I lifted, gained weight, and began fooling around with the 16# shot put. Weighing 180#, I managed to put the bigger shot put just over 49'. Later I was shipped to the SW Pacific where I operated a landing barge for CG Unit 211—one of several construction units building Loran stations from Alaska to Okinawa.

Returning home after nearly four years in the Coast Guard, I soon fell back into my prewar routine: carpentry, gymnastics, and working with my now badly warped, wooden javelins. It was different, however, as I was married and had a small daughter to care for. Thus when the GI Bill was passed, I decided to go to college. At first, it was just part-time to earn an Associate of Arts degree. With that in hand, I made an appointment with Jess Hill, athletic director at the University of Southern California. I told him that I wanted to be a javelin thrower, and he, in turn, introduced me to the legendary Trojan coach, Mr. Dean Cromwell.

Actually, I started training for two sports—my first love gymnastics and my new love, track and field. One day while I was working with the javelin coach Cromwell came to watch me. In ten minutes, he taught me more about the javelin than all of the clinicians and coaches since. "Always keep your hand above your shoulder . . . keep the point by your eye . . . run up and stop abruptly and then pull. Throwing the javelin is something like pulling a tree from the ground by it roots," he said. "You take hold of a root, turn so that your back is toward the tree, pull hard, and throw the thing over your shoulder."

Mr. Cromwell always wore a suit, a hat, and bow tie. He referred to each of his athletes as "Mr. Champion," even me on the one and only day that he ever gave me coaching advice. I was deeply impressed by this great man. It was with keen regret that I had to drop out of track and field to give more time to my studies and my responsibilities at home. I did, however, continue in gymnastics where I was a two-time NCAA champion, All American, and record holder in the rope climb.

After earning a B.S. degree from USC, I returned as a part-time graduate student, while teaching health education and coaching girls' basketball and boys' track and field at a private high school. In 1950, I moved to Seattle Pacific College where I taught courses in exercise science and coached basketball, cross-country, and track and field. While the college had limited facilities and equipment, I had freedom to do whatever I wished. In those early years, potential track and field athletes were recruited from gym classes and intramural events. The annual Thanksgiving "turkey trot" proved to be a positive source for middle distance potential.

For a reason unknown to me now, I focused my attention on getting relay teams into the Drake Relays. To subsidize trips to this Midwest meet, we contracted to drive new cars from Detroit to Seattle—one year we raised "a mile of pennies" (figuratively) to help subsidize our trip to Drake. To get there we would purchase one-way train tickets to Minneapolis, take a bus to Detroit, pick up our cars, and drive to Des Moines, home of Drake University. We never had enough money for sleepers, so we sat up, getting off at the long stops to loosen up on the train platform. While the trip back to Seattle was tedious at best, we always took a circuitous route, visiting such disparate places as the Painted Desert in Arizona and Glacier National Park, Montana. Our best showing at Drake was in 1954 when we placed 2nd in the 2-mile relay.

Although we were competing nationally, we had difficulty getting into track and field meets at home. To resolve this problem, I volunteered to serve on the district NAIA committee and assist with the first regional track and field meet. The strategy worked, as several SPU athletes qualified for the National NAIA Championship meet in Abilene, TX, where SPU junior, Ben Moring won the 880y. The following year we were welcomed into the Pacific NW track and field community. We were particularly successful in the sprints, middle distance events, and in cross-country. Our success in the sprints likely led to a telephone call from a high school teacher that was to be a nudge in a radically new direction for my professional career.

Jim Lord, a teacher at Renton High School, then a suburb south of Seattle, observed a 15-year-old girl racing against and beating boys from the high school track and field team. He called me to see if I would be interested in working with this obviously talented girl. His call posed a serious dilemma for my family and me. I was teaching a full load of college course work and coaching basketball, as well as working on my master's degree. In addition, all of my previous training had taught me that girls were too fragile for serious training and competition. Yet I had coached girls' basketball, and albeit an essentially stationary game, none of the girls with whom I had worked appeared to have been traumatized by the experience. Why not give this a try? At least time the girl and see if she was for real.

Two nights later, I met Jim and Marcia Cosgrove on the college track. It was October and dark when Marcia was ready to run. The plan was for her to run 100 yards, starting when I fired my pistol and running toward a Colman lantern at my end of the track. I fired into the night, and she came sprinting past—her time was 11.4. Assuming this to be fairly good, I asked her to "jog back, wait for the gun, and try it again." We repeated the exercise and Marcia's time was the same. It was then that I noted that she was running in bare feet. She stood there—an eager, excited, and obviously talented kid. I agreed, with conditions, to be her coach.

In January of 1956, Marcia entered her first track and field meet—the NAAU Indoor Championship meet, which was held in Washington, DC. What an introduction to the world of women's track and field, an inexperienced girl running in her first meet against the likes of Mae Faggs, Isabel Daniels, Lucinda Williams, and Margaret Mathews. Marcia placed 3rd in both the 100 and 220, proving that she was for real. Subsequently, we trained with a higher level of intensity, usually after my college men had left the track. I was both her coach and training partner.

In August, Marcia made her bid for the Olympic team, first by competing in the NAAU Championship meet at Philadelphia and later the Olympic trials in Washington, DC. She performed well in the AAU meet and appeared to be a strong contender for a place on the Olympic team. However, the Olympic trials proved to be anything but an equal opportunity event. Initially, we were informed sprinters would be chosen by their performance against the stop watches, not according to how they placed. Young and naive, I expected this strange rule to prevail, and when Marcia posted the third fastest time (11.3) in the 100, we assumed that she was on the team. We returned to our hotel for lunch and rest prior to the preliminary heats of the 220y.

When we returned to the track, we were shocked to discover that the rules had changed. Sprinters now had to race again, and this time team selection was to be by head-to-head competition. Without adequate warm up, Marcia ran two additional heats of the 100y and one qualifying heat of the 220y, before the finals of the latter event. When the results were posted, Marcia was listed as fourth in both events, though I was certain then and am convinced to this day that she placed second in the 220y. We were devastated. I did not know what to do. With whom was I to submit a formal protest? Someone suggested that I talk with Dan Farris, Chairman of the National AAU. After hearing my story, Mr. Farris looked at me, smiled, and walked away.

The following day the "Seattle Post Intelligencer," a major Seattle newspaper ran a headline that clearly delineated my first significant experience with the AAU. The headline asked, "What Did They Do Too Our Marcia?"

If my memory serves me correctly, the chairman of the selection committee for the 1956 Women's Olympic Track and Field Team was an AAU person who was affiliated with wrestling. I was convinced then and have had no reason to change my mind over the years that the team had already been selected prior to the trials. When the pressure was on from the Seattle P-I and political leaders in our state, Marcia was later invited to travel to Los Angeles for a "run off to select members for the relay team." Yet the damage had

Ken Foreman

been done. She had lost her steam, and she wisely (I believe) chose not to go.

One consequence of the notoriety that we received was that people began to look at me as if I were a sprint coach. A father of a local high school football player came to me and asked if it were possible to improve sprint speed, and if so, would I be interested in conducting speed training classes for high school athletes? That father, a University of Washington professor of physiology, convinced me that such a class would attract many high school boys and could be a positive adjunct to their development and performance. An article appearing in the Seattle Times on July 26, 1956, delineated the aim of my class as "to run faster easier" using such things as relaxation, varied stride cadence, over speed sprinting, and specialized strength training. More than 70 boys attended that class, and some of them later (not necessarily because of) became professional athletes.

I returned to graduate school at USC in 1957, perhaps wiser, somewhat disenchanted from my brief encounter with women's track and field, but with many questions stemming from experience in the trenches. In short, I wanted to learn more about the female athlete and perhaps write my dissertation on neuromuscular factors governing the enhancement of speed. My disenchantment took on a new dimension when no one seemed to be interested in my real life experience of working with female athletes. Even worse, I was to encounter the old line that females were too fragile to train and participate in a highly competitive athletic arena and my major professor advised against my pursuing the question of speed, saying, "You will never find a committee willing to risk their reputation on the thesis that runners can improve their natural speed."

On balance, however, graduate school was a positive experience, helping me make the choice between construction/building and teaching/coaching. I was excited and ready to return to Seattle Pacific where the president assured me he was in favor of exploring an intercollegiate athletic program for our female students.

New Beginnings

It was weeks after the devastating loss to Marie Mulder before Doris and I were able to talk objectively about past and future hopes and expectations. When we did, it became startlingly clear how naive we had been to expect an athlete to perform at her peak when impacted by the emotional stress of getting married, attending graduate school, adjusting to the hostility of a jealous school administrator, etc. I also became acutely aware that while my graduate training had been intellectually challenging, it had not prepared me in anyway to coach a talented, female distance runner. My graduate professors were among the best in their areas of specialization: Dr. Lawrence Morehouse, Exercise Physiology, Dr. John Cooper, Kinesiology-Biomechanics, and Dr. John D. Lawther, Sport Psychology. Yet none had anything to say about the female athlete. It was abundantly clear that if Doris and I were to be successful, we would have to find answers to our questions by mucking along in the trenches.

One afternoon, while jogging through leaves piled high on a favorite trail, Doris said to me "I have heard that Jim Ryun trains twice a day . . . maybe if it is good enough for him it would be good for me." Obviously not significant today, it was then. No female runner whom we knew was running twice a day. We continued to jog; I listened and agreed to meet Doris at our Green Lake course the following morning. That single event was a turning point in the running career of Doris Brown (Heritage).

In February of 1965, all-of-my runners, male and female alike, joined Doris for an early morning run. Not only did we train twice a day, we intensified workloads setting a goal of 50 miles of running training each week. (Appendix A) Because of Doris' vision and fortitude, we never looked back, and that is the rest of the story.

The first test of our revised training program came March 6 at the British Columbia Mid-Winter Games, where Doris won two events—300m (41.8) and 600m (1:42.9). (Time for the 300m was submitted for a US national record.) We were encouraged by results in British Columbia; training continued to go well. Doris ran her first 800m of the season, winning at the Vancouver Relays (May 8) with a time of 2:17.0. She lowered her seasons best to 2:14.1 while winning the BC International 800m (June14). Doris was ready, we believed, for a return match with rising star Marie Mulder, but alas, it was not to be. One week later, Doris injured a hamstring while doing speed work, knocking her out of the NAAU Championship meet.

Doris entered into rehabilitation, stretching, lifting, and swimming with the same zeal she manifest on the track. At the risk of hyperbole, it can be said that her commitment to getting back on the track was beyond comprehension. She was driven; therapists could not believe the intensity with which she worked. A note in my training log dated July 18, 1965, reads, "Doris is as tenacious in rehab as on the track . . . have seen her in a swimming pool early in the morning steam rising from her bright red body, kicking as if her life depended on it. She will cling to a chinning bar, knuckles turning blue, straining for one more rep."

While not fully recovered, Doris insisted that she run for the hometown crowd in Seattle's Highland Games (August 14). She won both the 880y and mile with 30 minutes rest (2:16.1/5:21.6). The remainder of August was committed to active rest, swimming, cycling, and hiking. We resumed training the first Monday of September, our focus now on winning the National Championships in cross-country.

In 1965, we determined that cross-country would encompass 16–17 weeks of training and competition, beginning the 2nd week of August and continuing through the National Championship meet in late November. We trained Monday-Saturday, with Sunday a full day of rest. Blessed with a wide variety of exceptionally good training areas, we trained at a different site every day. One was an arboretum encircled with miles of firm, undulating trails. Another was a lakeshore with long stretches of grass parkway and a wooded peninsula with towering, first-growth fir, cedar, and hemlock. We trained at an old fort where we could run for miles through open fields, down steep grades, along grassy ridges. Once a week, we trained in a large park with rolling hills and long, easy grades. A favorite activity in the park was bounding onto and off picnic tables, fireboxes, and boulders that were strewn about. (We would call that plyometrics today.) The least favorite, though likely one of the most important workout was a one-mile loop with 100+ stairs at either end.

Saturdays were reserved for fun things like team hikes. Before the trails were closed by snow, we carried packs to our favorite high lakes, set up camp, and would then run at elevations between 4000'-6000'. When snow arrived in the high country, our weekend ritual was running a step down— 6 miles along the shore of Lake Washington. Target times were determined by conditioning, with the late-season goal of running the first mile in 7 minutes, the second mile in 6 minutes, and mile three in 5 minutes 30 seconds. After two miles of recovery running over wooded terrain, runners ran a maximum effort, mile six. My records show that Doris completed this work out on several occasions by running her final mile under 5 minutes. (Perhaps it is noteworthy that for more than 30 years, working with university runners, Doris has used this training activity as a predictor of performance potential and readiness for national competition.)

In retrospect, it is safe to say that we trained a great

deal on hills. In fact, members of the Falcon Track Club took pride in the fact that no one was going to beat them going up hill. While Doris was toughest on the hill, several other Falcon Track Club runners were hard to beat on a hilly course. These included Vicki Foltz, a member of two US International Cross-Country teams, and Trina Hosmer, who put bricks in her pack when doing hill work. (Trina was a member of the US Winter Olympic cross-country ski team the same year she ran with the US cross-country team in San Sebastian, Spain.) Linda Mayfield, Falcon Track Club and Seattle Pacific runner, who developed her strength on hills by running home from high school. (Linda lived in a cabin several miles up a dirt road in Cave Junction, Oregon.) Kathy McIntyre, Beth Bonner, Maria Stearns, and Judy Oliver—tough competitors on hills—were members of US International cross-country teams.

Doris was fit, strong on hills, ready to run in the 1965 National Cross-Country meet, but tough luck was winner again. The week before the national meet Doris broke out with chicken pox and was home in bed when Sandra Knott won the championship race.

A longtime tradition for Seattle Pacific and Falcon Track Club runners was participation in a season ending, so-called "mud meet." The latter provided opportunity for all athletes to post performance marks that reflected the quality of their fall training. Recovered from the chicken pox, Doris ran the mile in 5.03.7, with an intermediate time 4:44.8 at the 1500m mark in the 1965 "mud meet." We were cautiously elated, as this was the fastest that Doris had ever run the mile, but perplexed as she had done so at the end of cross-country and not during track season when she might have been specifically training for the event.

Several days passed before I would return to the apparent contradiction. A highly conditioned female, running a faster mile on a generalized (cross-country) training program than on a schedule focused on specificity—was this an inexplicable happening, or did it represent some unknown factor where females were concerned? In an effort to resolve my quandary, I looked at "mud meet" marks representing men as well as women, attained over a period of five years. In so doing, I discovered that our better female runners often ran faster 1-mile and 2-mile times in the fall-winter cycle than they did in spring and summer. All of the men had their best marks in the spring.

The question then was this: Does this finding have significance, or is it an artifact having little relevance to the way female runners ought to train for middle distance and distance events? I was inclined to think that if this happened to a female runner who trained as hard as Doris, it must have some hidden significance. After careful study of Doris' training records, I concluded that the quality of her performance was directly related to the quality and quantity of her aerobic training.

Prior to 1966, there were few opportunities for girls and women to compete indoors. Our training plan during those years was to rest following the "mud meet" and run when weather permitted, returning to the track the first week of February. We now needed to test a new assumption; would added aerobic training in the winter-spring training schedule enhance performance on the track? The answer came in a startling way at the Argodome in Vancouver, BC, on February 19, 1966.

I now know that what we observed with our top women in the '60s has great significance. Female distance runners, who have less muscle mass than male runners, have a more difficult time maintaining their aerobic base than do men. When female runners change their focus from aerobic training to speed and power, the resulting loss in aerobic capacity has a deleterious impact on performance in aerobically weighted activities. In short, it is my strong belief that female distance runners need to continue with one or two long runs each week during track season if they intend to achieve their maximum potential.

"THE BE SPECKLED GIRL WITH PIG TAIL FLYING"

The athletic domain is replete with certainties: uniforms, specialized equipment, facilities, rules, regulations, etc. Yet there are uncertainties, and they likely are an important attraction for participants and spectators as well. For many years, a great uncertainty in track and field was if and when a runner (male) would break the 4-minute barrier for the mile. On May 6, 1954, Roger Bannister, medical student, did just that on a wet and windy track, breaking the barrier with a time of 3:59.4. Bannister was an instant hero—legend in the annals of track and field.

In stark contrast, on February 19, 1966, it was not widely known that 5 minutes was the mile barrier for women, or that a Canadian schoolgirl was thought to be the most likely athlete to break the 5-minute mile barrier. However, for those who knew, the Canadian Indoor Championships were assumed to be a time and place where a world record run was a real possibility. So certain were meet promoters of the possibility of a world record in the women's mile that they contracted with Ron Delanay, a highly respected, former world record holder to announce the race.

The expected winner of this indoor mile was a talented, young Canadian whose name was Roberta Pico, but the eventual winner was an anonymous runner from Seattle. She had broken the 5-minute barrier for women; she was now known as "the be speckled girl with pig tail flying."

This is how Doris, the anonymous runner, came to be a world record holder and winner of the mile run in what was expected to be a Pico spectacular. A friend in the BC Track and Field Federation called to inform me that meet promoters were looking for distance runners who could provide competition for Canadian superstar Roberta Pico. He said I should contact the promoters to see if Doris was considered to be a strong enough runner to be competitive. My call to the promoters of this event yielded positive results as two Falcon TC runners were invited to participate. The two were Doris Brown and Patty Engberg, better known as a highly successful cross-country skier.

In the weeks leading up to the BC event, we revised our training program yet again—more miles/week and specific pace training aimed at running a 4:57 mile. Doris had completed course work for her master's degree and was pain free for the first time in months, permitting us to train harder than at any time in the past. Markers that we used to measure fitness indicated that Doris was ready to run a strong mile race, perhaps even win. However, when we arrived at the Agrodome, our confidence was sorely tested. There apparently was a mix up. Our names were not on the gate list and we were informed we could not enter the building without a ticket. I was frustrated, ready to walk away, when my friend, Lloyd Swindells, executive member of the Vancouver Olympic Club arrived at the pass gate. He assured the "keeper of the list" that Doris and Patty were indeed scheduled to run, and we were permitted to enter the competitive arena.

As it turned out, getting in was the least of our concerns. We were unable to locate an athletes' changing room, did not have a schedule of events, and thus could not properly warm up—we were ignored. When entries in the women's mile were called to the start, the stadium announcer introduced Roberta Pico as the "runner most likely to break the 5-minute mile barrier and Canada's hope for a new world record." Several other runners, including Doris and Patty seemed to be anonymous participants in a Pico event.

At the crack of the starters' gun, Pico immediately took the lead, setting a world record pace. The stadium was electric with expectation all eyes were on the front-runner as Doris worked her way through the pack. On lap 3, she was running on Pico's shoulder. Around and around they went, Pico seemly in command of the race. By lap 5, the crowd was on its feet; Pico pressed the pace, and Doris doggedly held on. Our race plan was for Doris to follow for nine laps, and then, if possible, to pass. However, to my shock, Doris passed Roberta on lap 7. As she took the lead, I was yelling like a fool, "Don't pass! Don't pass!" . . . and Delaney was searching for her name.

As he scrambled to see who this interloper was, he said something about Pico "letting her (Doris) run herself out." By lap 10 (11 lap race), it was obvious that Doris was going to win, and Delaney, who still did not know her name, called out, "She is going like a bomb . . . this Be Speckled Runner With Pig Tail Flying is going like a bomb. She is going to win!" And win she did, setting two world records in her first international, indoor race.

That February evening, when we arrived at the Agrodome, we believed that Doris could win, and that she could run the mile under 5:00 and had set our lap splits for a 4:57 effort. We also had an incentive; Pico had beaten most of the top American runners in the past several weeks. Her coach was reported to have said, "She could beat any runner in North America at any distance between 600 and a mile."

Following is our race plan and the actual lap splits:

Race plan	Actual	
27	24	
54	49	
1:21	1:15	
1:48	1:45	
2:15	2:13	2:28 at 880y
2:42	2:43	
3:09	3:10	Doris passed Pico
3:36	3:35	
4:03	4:00	
4:30	4:25	4:33.3 at 1500m
4:57	4:52	

The morning after the BC event, the "Vancouver Sun" ran a headline that read "Indoor Meet Smashing." The accompanying article noted that the "Canadian Indoor Championships at the Agrodome produced five world records . . . Strangely, perhaps, the world records were all established by female athletes," one of whom "was named the outstanding female athlete, 24 year old Mrs. Brown, broke two world records while running the mile in 4:52, 11.6 seconds faster than the previous standard. En route Brown also broke the record for 1500 meters with a time of 4:33.3 . . . Doris wasn't even the favorite before the race. That role was occupied by 16-year-old Roberta Pico of Toronto, and naturally, all eyes were on her at the start of the race . . . Brown was running the first three-quarters of the mile slightly behind Miss Pico. Then, with four laps remaining, Doris spurted past the surprised Ontario girl and opened up a lead, to the amazement of all."[4]

Eric Whitehead wrote, "The quiet girl in the white-framed horn-rims dazzled the Agrodome throng with a world-record run of 4:52 in the mile and also smashed the women's 1500-meters mark en-route."[5]

We were elated, almost giddy as we drove back to Seattle, but our mood would soon change, as few people on our side of the border seemed to be aware of what Doris had accomplished. In sad contrast to the positive recognition received in Vancouver, Doris was viewed, as she had been prior to her record-breaking run as that strange blond girl who ran around Green Lake while rational people slept. When the Sports Information Director at Seattle Pacific University made calls to local news outlets, he discovered that a world record by a woman was not that important in our town.

Publications like "Track and Field News" did not cover women's events and the only seriously interested publisher was Vince Reel, editor of the "pink sheet" called "Track

Talk." It was Vince who alerted the world of women's athletics that a serious confrontation was heating up—Doris, the world, indoor-mile record holder, would soon be facing a precocious, teenage Marie Mulder, who held the American record for the 1500m run.

The Vancouver experience proved to be a turning point for Doris and me. It had become clear that a fine line often separates failure and success. Had we walked away from the little man at the pass gate and returned home, as I was tempted to do, all of our training and planning would have been for naught—failure of a sort, but having stayed and won, we were high achievers—our efforts a success. We also were wiser as to the tenuous nature of success—it sometimes being relative at best.

Perhaps the most important lesson learned from our experience was an Ed Temple truth: "This thing would either drive us up, or it would drive us down." Setting a world record called us to a higher standard. We were beginning to understand what it would take to be the best and more importantly, what we had to do to be the best and we were determined to make it happen.

On April 16, Doris ran an 880y during the men's mile in a dual track and field meet between Seattle Pacific and Portland State University. According to the post meet news release, "Mrs. Brown was clocked by two watches at 2:09.8 and one watch at 2:09.7."[6] This was her fastest 880y ever and an indication that we were on target with our revised training program. However, as so often was a reality in the athletic domain, Doris suddenly was unable to complete her expected workload. According to our team physician, she likely had mononucleosis.

Dr. Keith Peterson advised us to back off depending on Doris' sense of well-being as our guide regarding training and competition. Following a week of complete rest, Doris competed in the Vancouver Relays, setting a new stadium and relays record in the 880y, with the time 2:14.9 (5/6–7). One week later, at the Angels Invitational in Auburn, WA, Doris won the 880y in the time of 2:13.5. Following the Auburn meet, Doris took another week of complete rest. She resumed training, and on June 4, while competing in the Puget Sound AAU Championships, she accomplished an impressive, single-day performance by winning the 1500m in 4:31.2 (an unofficial world record), winning the 880y in 2:12.1 and running a 2:11.2 relay leg on our 4 x 880y team.

It was now obvious that Doris did not have mononucleosis, but rather a brief bout with a low-grade infection. Relieved by the new diagnosis, we turned down the screws, having Doris run one final race prior to the National Champions scheduled for July 1–3 in Frederick, MD. Running in the 7th annual Seattle Relays on June 18, Doris proved her readiness to meet Marie Mulder, defending national champion, posting an unofficial world record in the 1500m of 4:26.3, returning to the track after a 30-minute rest to win the 880y in 2:11.1.

In the fall of 1964, Marie Mulder, competing for Will's Spikettes, beat Doris in head-to-head competition on our home cross-country course. She was a true talent of our sport and considered by many to be the best of the best. Although Doris now had better performance marks than Marie, many persons in the track and field community considered Marie to be the better of the two. Thus Doris and I traveled to Frederick, Maryland, for the NAAU Championships, fully aware that we were assumed to be the challengers—not the runner to beat.

Prior to our leaving Seattle a sportswriter for the Seattle Times, interviewed Doris and she is quoted as saying, "I'm anxious to run against Marie . . . I've never been in better physical condition, but I'm holding my breath over injuries."[7]

Doris and I are not superstitious. But when she was

barely able to walk on our arrival at the Fredrick airport, I began to wonder if she had a premonition of things to come while talking to Dick Rockne. Her hamstrings had tightened up from the long airplane ride. Doris waited. I retrieved our baggage, and we caught a cab to our hotel. Thus began the saga of the ice and an accusation on the part of the bellboy that we "were holding a wild party in our hotel room."

When I called our team physician to ask for advice, he instructed me to fill a bathtub with cold water, put in lots of ice, and have Doris sit in the tub 15 minutes every hour until bedtime. "Repeat the process again in the morning," he said, "giving you two hours to get to the track, warm up, and run." Now that is a lot of sitting, requiring many bags of ice. When I continued to call the bellboy for ice, he informed the manager, and we had a visit from the front office.

I had a difficult time explaining to the hotel manager what was occurring in the bath room. It was similarly difficult trying to explain to fellow coaches why Doris was so red. There also was the problem of revealing to our competitors that Doris was hurting—so she and I just smiled and let her do her talking on the track.

In the early days of women's track and field, the names Jack Griffin, the Fredrick Track Club and the city of Fredrick, Maryland, were synonymous with excellence in our sport. Hosting both national and international events, the people of Fredrick were strong supporters of women's events. Thus the stands were filled for finals on a warm Saturday afternoon, with betting seemingly split evenly between Mulder and Brown to reign as middle distance queen.

In a race that surprised and shocked all in attendance, Doris, the front-runner, took the lead and ran away from the defending champion. She finished in 4:20.2 (67–2:17.3–3:29.1–4:20.2), 80 meters ahead of Mulder, who ran 4:36.6—one tenth of a second off her previous record.

Doris Brown now was leader of the pack; she was the

runner to beat, and that was a tough place to be! Nevertheless, Doris proved she was ready for the challenge. With less than week to recover from her record-breaking race at Fredrick, Doris led the Washington State women's team against a strong team from British Columbia, setting meet and personal best marks in the 440y and 880y respectively. Her winning times were 56.7 and 2:08.5. Doris led in both races, beating Karen Emery in the 880y by more than 100 yards. In the 440y, she beat Canadian Colleen Davis by 25 yards.

With one day of rest, Doris flew to Berkley to train with the U.S. Team for dual meets with Poland and Russia. The 1500m race was not scheduled for either meet, thus Doris was an alternate in the 880y. A last minute cancellation of both meets for political reasons resulted in an intersquad meet at Berkley on July 17. Finishing second behind Charlotte Cooke, Doris set a new personal best at 880 yards with the time of 2:05.1. One week later in a meet held in Los Angeles, Doris ran fourth in a blanket-finish of the 880y, equaling her time of 2:05.1 set the previous weekend.

After five years of frustration and a career plagued by injury, Doris was beginning to fulfill her dream of being an outstanding runner. (A slow-to-heal metatarsal fracture hampered her performances 1962–64, as did a pulled hamstring muscle on the eve of the 1965 AAU Nationals.) But 1966 was a different story, starting with her world record run at the BC Agrodome on February 19, she had won every major race in which she participated during a period of seven months. In addition to her indoor mile record, she had set an American and a world record in the 1500 meter (4:20.2) and a personal best in the 880 (2:05.1).

There were five months remaining in what had, thus far, been the best year of her running life. We were excited; Doris ended the track and field season pain free, and her first love, cross-country, was just a few short weeks away.

Then "Wham!" As so often happens when one is training on the edge, an accident occurred. On the first day, of the first week, of the fall semester, Doris fell and separated her shoulder while demonstrating soccer skills to her students at Kellogg Junior High School. I was devastated, but not Doris, who in spite of her injury resumed training with her arm in a sling.

Running with her arm in a sling, Doris entered her first cross-country meet of the 1966 season on Oct. 8, a 3-mile race against college/university men. Her time of 17:14 was a personal best on the hilly, Woodland Park course. Two weeks later, she ran in the Canadian National Cross-Country Championships at Vancouver, BC, arm in a sling. She won the 1.5-mile event in a meet record time of 7:25.6. On November 19, Doris won the Pacific Northwest Cross-Country Championships on a soggy, 1.5-mile course, in the time of 7:46. She was ready, we believed, for her a rematch with Marie Mulder, who was winner of their last head-to-head, cross-country race in the fall of 1964.

The National AAU Cross-Country Championships were held in St. Louis, Missouri, on November 26. The temperature was 60 degrees. Rain and wind whipped across the hilly course as the dominant distance runners of that era came to the starting line. In addition to Marie Mulder, these were Nathalie Rocha, Cheryl Pedlow, Lori Schutt, Pat Cole, Sandra Knott, and Falcon Track Club teammate, Vicki Foltz. At the gun, Doris moved immediately into the lead, staying with her now-familiar race strategy; she pressed the pace from the first step to the last. Her winning time was 7:51.1— Mulder was 2nd in 8:29 and Rocha 3rd in 8:35. (Splits were 2:12.9–4:58.7–7:51.1.)

Doris ran one more race in 1966, a somewhat reluctant participant in the so-called Autumn Games (a track and field event hosted by the Angels Track Club, perhaps best known for Patty Van Wolvelaere, American record holder in the 80-meter hurdles). Doris' times were 2:12.0 and 4:55.3, achieved with less than an hours' recovery. Both marks were remarkably similar to her splits in the cross-country championships contested two weeks earlier. We did not know it then, but the achievements of the 1966 season were but hints of the success that Doris would have in 1967 and a glimpse of the stature that she would accrue as an internationally recognized distance runner. Indeed, her performance on the track and in cross-country was finally attracting attention in the larger world: coaches, competitors, members of the press, even commercial interests (unprecedented at the time). That is the next episode in the running career of Doris Brown.

Ken Foreman

CHASING THE GOLDEN FLEECE

About a week before the National Cross-Country Championships, I received a telephone call from a representative of a well-known shoe company asking if he could meet with Doris and me to discuss a shoe contract. Naïve, flustered, I asked the shoe man to call again, when we returned from St. Louis, and we would arrange a time to talk. He called, and we decided that the meeting ought to occur on our track during a training session for the final outdoor meet of the year, the so-called Autumn Games hosted by Ron Sorkness and his Angels Track Club.

On the afternoon of our appointment, a taxi stopped at the entrance to the track, and a man in suit and tie climbed out. He stood looking, did not move further than 5' from the taxi, causing me to run to the gate to greet him and introduce him to our champion, Doris Brown. Turning from the track toward me, he asked, "Is this where you always train?" The inference being, *Are you here on this wet cinder oval just to meet me? Surely, you have a better place to train.*

I responded, "Yes, this is our college track."

The shoe man turned, looked again at our facility, turned back toward me, and said, "No one of any significance will ever come from this track." He climbed back in the taxi and drove off.

When Doris arrived at Seattle Pacific College, our track and field team trained on a cinder track. Constructed by volunteer help, a war surplus bulldozer, and a student-owned truck, the track remains as a community recreational site to this day. It was never quite finished, because we destroyed the truck when hauling hot clinkers from the coal-fired furnaces at our cinder source. The college track was my home for more than four decades. Doris trained on that track during her entire running career, as did Olympians Karen Frisch (Germany), Bente Moe (Norway) Sharon Walker, Pam Spencer, and Lorna Griffin, and more than 20 US International Team members and 165 NCAA All Americans.

Over the years, I have pondered the shoe man's assumption that a location, a particular situation, is the primary determinant of achievement—athletic or any other kind. Recently, while conducting a clinic, a young man said to me, "I could be really good if I had a decent track to train on." (Most tracks here on the big island of Hawaii are pumice, a kind of volcanic ash.) Once again, the specter of the shoe man was this boy on to some truth that is fundamental to peak performance, or was he, in the words of my friend Dr. Paul Ward, "chasing the golden fleece"?

When I first turned out for track more than 65 years ago, things were vastly different than they are today. Our high school track and all field event surfaces were either cinder or dirt. Sprinters dug holes in the track to serve as starting blocks, jumpers landed in piles of wet wood shavings, and those who dared vaulted with bamboo poles. (Dutch Warmerdam, perhaps the greatest pole vaulter of all time, set many world records from the end of a bamboo pole.)

My high school coach was a PE teacher who worked alone, primarily with the sprints and hurdles. Those of us who participated in field events learned from upper classman, passing along our skills as we had learned.

Much has changed over the years, most for the good, including better equipment and facilities, improved coaching, expanded competitive opportunities, performance marks as well. Yet I continue to wonder if there aren't other, less obvious factors at work where performance is concerned? During track season I regularly scour the sports page for results of track and field meets; I've done this for more than 60 years.

Each time I do so, I note an apparent relationship between school-size, quality of competition, and performance marks. The question raised in my mind is, what can be attributed to the size of an institution, and what to a level of expectation?

When one talks with Doris Brown Heritage or reads the record of her achievements, it soon becomes obvious that she had big dreams and powerful expectations from the first day that she started to run. When Doris stepped onto the track at the Agrodome to run against Roberta Pico, **she believed she would win—and she did.**

Later, in Barry Wales, she "heard them (her opponents) breathing heavily." She passed and she won. In all the years that I worked with Doris, she never once asked how much or when we would finish. She never questioned; rather she went out and did what she was expected to do.

Lorna Griffin, two-time Olympian in the shot and discus, former member of our Seattle Pacific University team, was born on a diary farm near Corvallis, Montana. At an early age, while watching her brothers participate in basketball, football, and track and field, she developed an interest in and an appreciation for sport. She also loved to work with her father in the field, taking pride in the fact that she was as good as any other hired hand. Lorna loved PE during high school and wanted to be a member of an athletic team, choosing track and field because it was the only athletic activity for girls. During high school, she competed in a variety of events, excelling in the throws and winning the Class B State Championship in the shot, discus, and javelin.

Lorna's high school experience was typical for a small, rural school in the 1970s with limited coaching and inadequate equipment and facilities. She credits her brother for her early success. He purchased her implements, poured a concrete slab on which she trained, and was her coach. When describing her situation, Lorna writes, "It was a little bit of hassle to throw in the pasture because my discus would often slide into the cow pies. Also, a near by irrigation canal seemed to swallow up my discus."[8] After high school Lorna chose to attend Flat Head Community College, located in Kalispell, Mt., where a young, aggressive man named Neil Eliason coached track and field. While at Flat Head, Lorna qualified for the Olympic trials, placing 4th in the discus. She transferred to Seattle Pacific in the fall of 1977, joining Marcia Mecklenburg and Julia Hansen to form the strongest collegiate throwing team in America. All trained on the shoe man's inadequate facility.

A final word about Lorna Griffin, the winter before she moved to Southern California to work with Dr. Paul Ward, she asked me to make a pact with her that we would train six days every week regardless of the weather and get to the best meets in the country. There were days that winter when I poured gasoline on the discus pad to burn off the ice so Lorna could throw, and there were days when it rained so hard that she could only work on her hip punch, but we trained every day as agreed, competing in the best meets that we could find. One day during a training session, I stopped Lorna, saying "I need to clean something off the cement before you throw again." Taking a towel, I stooped to wipe the surface clean and was shocked to see that the spot was blood!

When I stood up I asked Lorna to show me the bottom of her shoe—she did as asked, revealing a quarter size hole through her shoe, through her sock, and into her foot, all from the constant turning, turning, turning essential for her event. If I had not stopped her, she would be turning still. This humble, determined, gifted athlete became the best discus thrower in America. She learned to throw in a cow pasture, and she seldom had enough money to purchase new shoes.

Other highly skilled athletes also developed their skills

on so-called inadequate facilities—or developed their technique almost by chance. Hurdle guru Wilbur Ross proudly states he produced an Olympic champion who trained on the lawn in front of the college administration building.[9] It is reported that Perry O' Brien, testing a theory posited by his kinesiology professor, Dr. John Cooper, developed the O' Brien technique by throwing his shot in the backyard of his home. Dick Fosberry developed the universally used Fosberry flop while fooling around with scissors jumps into bags of foam on the Lewis and Clark College track.

During the protracted period of team preparation for the 1988 Olympics, Dave Rodda and I were advised on several occasions to seek the counsel of a particular coach having "special knowledge" about the preparation of sprinters and hurdlers. The fact was, he happened to be married to and coached a very special athlete. The idea of special knowledge was an illusion similar to the belief that success lies in having a better track to train on.

I am not arguing that effective coaching, good equipment, facilities, and quality of competition is unimportant where athletic success is concerned. Rather, I am suggesting there is no such thing as a "silver bullet." State high school champions, NCAA champions, or nationally and internationally ranked athletes, Olympians come in all sizes and shapes. They come from a myriad of places. Some facilities were good, others not so good. (On a recent visit to Russia, I observed grass and weeds growing through the track facility at the National Training Center.) These athletes do, however, have one thing in common; they are physically gifted, and they are committed to be the best that they can be.

In short, it isn't so much the track one trains on, as it is how one trains on the track that she or he has to train on. Almost any place, I firmly believe, can be a launching pad for greatness!

"I Heard their Labored Breathing–i Passed–i Won"

I can see him still a tall man in suite and tie hair slicked back exuding smug superiority. He put a microphone in her face and asked Doris, "Do you actually believe you can win in England? Haven't you heard of the Lincoln Twins?" Doris looked the BBC announcer in the eye and said, "Yes, I know how strong they are, but I came here to compete, and I expect do my best." That exchange occurred on the starting line of the first-ever International Cross-Country race for women.

Doris and I looked forward to the 1967 season with great anticipation, but did not have a clue what a life-changing event was on the horizon. This chapter includes heretofore unreported information about a season and a race that created a legend and changed women's distance running forever.

Our first scheduled competition in 1967 was the Seattle Indoor to be held on February 4—a competitive event from which women had previously been excluded. Doris performed brilliantly for the packed arena. In his column, George S. Meyers described the response of spectators, writing "a tumultuous, standing ovation greeted Mrs. Brown as the petite, blond junior-high-school teacher snapped the tape in 2:08.5, a tenth of a second under the world record set a year ago at Albuquerque by Zsuaza Szabo of Hungry."[10]

One week later (2/11/67), Doris ran in the Times Indoor Games at the Los Angeles Sports Arena. Glenn White referred to the event as one in which "Records [were]

Doomed." He noted "The girls get their moment of glory in the 880y with indoor record holder Doris Brown (2:08.5) dueling with Charlotte Cooke, who boasts the fastest outdoor time for an American . . . 2:03.5."[11]

My recollection of that race is one of keen competition, with Doris winning, but the most memorable event (for me) occurred after the meet. Someone, I do not remember who, invited Doris and me to accompany meet officials to the Brown Derby restaurant in Hollywood for a post-meet dinner celebration. Arriving, we were truly impressed by the obvious affluence—more impressed still when the maitre d' showed us to our table. There sat a diminutive blonde girl in Falcon Track Club warm-ups who was the center of attraction. Soon a waiter arrived, explained the menu, left for a time, and returned to take our orders.

This is the Brown Derby, famous for guests and steaks. Smiling at her, the waiter asked, "Have you decided, Miss Champion?"

Smiling back, Doris responded, "A chocolate milk shake please." I would give a hundred dollars to have a picture of the look on that waiters face. I laughed so hard I had difficulty eating my prime rib and baked potato.

(After reading my working manuscript, Doris sent me the following note regarding her view of the Brown Derby story. "It's true, except the reason isn't clear and may be of interest. I had not consumed a milk shake for several years—it was to be saved for a special occasion connected with goals. That night was the night for the reward! I still feel that sort of thing doesn't determine health or excellence, but for me and others, I knew those small denials aided in the fun of accomplishment. When there are things out there in life you still desire, life is more fun than always getting what you want on the immediate spot—bridging the gap between desire and fulfillment as you taught us.)

The following week (2/16/67), we retuned to the

Agrodome in Vancouver, BC to run in the Achilles International Indoor Meet. This time spectators knew Doris' name and afforded her the kind of emulation that had been bestowed on Roberta Pico one year earlier. Doris responded by setting another world indoor record with a time of 4:40.4, almost 12 seconds faster than she had run 12 months earlier.

Cumulative time	Lap splits
23	23
48	25
1:13	25
1:38	25
2:05	27
2:31	26
2:57	26
3:23	26
3:46	23
4:13	27
4:40.4	27.4
67.0-2:17.2-3:31.1-4:40.4	

What a difference a year would make. Doris and I returned to Seattle to find extensive coverage of her outstanding performance in both local newspapers. The Seattle Post Intelligencer ran a headline "DORIS AND DYROL TRIUMPH." (Dyrol Burleson was a world class mile runner from the University of Oregon) The accompanying article described her return to Vancouver as "a world record setting effort before an overflow crowd of 3,710 . . . Doris Brown of Seattle did the expected . . . and then some . . . by smashing her women's world record in the indoor mile with a superb 4:40.4 clocking." The writer stated further that Doris' win "helped to salve the disappointment of the heralded mile, won by Dyrol Burleson while Keino (Kipchoge) and Clark (Ron) were nowhere near the front."[12]

The exact circumstances are not clear to me now, but

shortly after returning from the Vancouver meet, Doris and I were contacted by meet officials in Barry, Wales, inviting Doris to run in the first International Cross-Country race for women. We were, of course, elated. I immediately called the office of the AAU to ask how we should respond to the invitation and the boondoggle was on! Informed that we must first apply for a sanction to participate in a foreign country and then told that funding for such a venture was not available, I was passed off to a Colonel Lipscomb whom I was informed I could find at the forthcoming AAU Indoor Championships to be conducted in New York City.

When I met with Colonel Lipscomb at Madison Square Garden, he acted as if he had not heard of the Barry event. I reminded him of my telephone conversation with members of the AAU staff, and his response was, "I'll call the office, you can contact me later tonight." Our meeting had not gone well, so I called my friend Royal Brougham, sports editor of the Seattle P-I to ask for his assistance. Mr. Brougham was well aware of AAU politics after our unfortunate experience with Marcia Cosgrove in 1956, and he agreed to use his influence on our behalf.

Later that evening when I met with Colonel Lipscomb, he was aware of the cross-country meet, and he had a formal authorization for our participation. However, when I asked if it was possible for me to secure an AAU Blazer so that I could formally represent the US, he curtly said, "No, you are own your own." He walked away leaving me standing along side the track.

Upon our return from New York, I reported to Mr. Brougham as he had requested, and after hearing my story, he said, "Let me make a few calls, and I will get back to you." Mr. Brougham and the P-I had supported Marcia Cosgrove and me during our run for the Olympics in 1956, and I was well aware that he knew his way around the financial community of our city. He made several telephone calls, gave me names and phone numbers, and sent me out to do the legwork. By the end of the day, we had the financial and technical support necessary for the trip to Wales.

At 4:30 P.M. on March 13, 1967, Doris and I flew out of Vancouver, BC, on Air Canada (The Empress of Buenos Aires), with intermediate stops at Edmonton and Calgary in route to Amsterdam. Transferring to KLM, we flew to London, took a bus and then a subway to Paddington station, where we boarded a train for the coastal town of Barry, Wales. Having been in the air or on the ground for more than 20 hours, we soon drifted into a deep sleep. When we awakened, we realized that we had missed our connection at Cardiff and were now on our way to some unknown place. We chugged onward, the train stopped, we disembarked, and we crossed over the tracks to catch a train headed back to Cardiff. When we finally arrived at the station at Barry, it was after midnight. An hour later, dizzy from wandering through narrow, crooked streets (length of the streets of Barry was determined by the distance a man could shoot an arrow—a medieval defense tactic in time of war), we were knocking on the front door of our hotel. There was no answer!

We knocked again and again and again. Finally there was a light inside and the door opened. The man who greeted us was dressed in formal attire. He proved to be the proprietor of the hotel. Solemn, yet with respect, he asked for identification, took our passports, and gave us keys to our rooms. We were five floors up, at the top of a winding stairway. The rooms were small, not much larger than my office at home, but that did not matter. We were desperate for sleep and just happy to have a clean bed.

The local club course for cross-country racing in Barry is at a place called Porthkerry Park. With minimal sleep, we set out to jog along the coast, find the park, run some easy strides, and return in time for breakfast. Arriving at the beach, we were amazed to discover that the shore, from cliff to sea, was nothing but rocks. It was, thus, a risky run to the park. At the park, we discovered another anomaly, unlike many of our well-manicured parks, this was a mostly unkempt place with meandering streams and watercress choked ponds. We negotiated the park and the many stone fences with care.

When we finally came to higher ground and a farmer's earthen trek, Doris took off on a run. Like a bird released from its cage, she flew across the ground. I could but watch her pigtail flying and struggled to keep up. Then she was gone, no trace of her flaxen hair to be seen.

Nearly breathless now, I plodded on. A farmhouse came into view. The pathway turned and there she was, digging into a pile of straw. Seeing me, she called out, "Look at what I have found!" I was looking at a sugar beet the size of a bowling ball. And before I could speak, Doris was biting into the side of the thing. My first thought was of the announcement at the start of the race some days later: "American Entry Too Sick to Run."

The following day we explored the racecourse, an eye-opening experience for an American coach and athlete. The start and finish were to be contested on the flat surface of a soccer complex, but much of the race was over a circuitous path through pastureland where cows were grazing in deep grass. We could only look from afar, as the fence was not yet cut and the course was closed to all but the cows.

Near one end of the pasture, we observed a swampy area—identified on the course map as a "ditch." This would become the focal point of our strategy for winning the forth-coming race. Doris would follow to the swampy area, push hard through the soggy ground, and then take the lead. If all went as planned, she would then have an unobstructed run to the finish line.

The day before the race, we were invited to accompany a group of runners on a bus tour to Afan Lido, Welsh National Training Center in the town of Abor Avon. Since it

Ken Foreman

was to be a leisurely drive along the coast and through magnificent rolling hills, we decided to go. Doris and I were first to board the bus and were in our seats when two men arrived, taking seats across from ours. They were obviously curious when seeing a female on the bus and asked who we were. I leaned back, and Doris, responding with a disarming smile, said, "I am Doris Brown, and who are you?"

I nearly fell from my seat when I heard the names of our companions.

What a great day it was: one small woman, her unknown coach, and a bus full of very famous men. During our trip, the men asked many questions, and Doris charmed them all with her ready responses and humble demeanor. All of these great distance runners were surprised . . . some were even shocked when Doris told them that she trained twice daily and often ran as many as 120 miles a week. It is an assumption, but I believe that some who scoffed at such a claim—a little girl running 120 miles a week—became believers on race day.

The road to Abor Avon brushes against the rugged coast at a place called Merthyr Mahr. The driver pulled off at a scenic point so we could get a better view. A rushing stream entered the sea nearby. Tall green waves washed high onto the sand dunes. Then we saw him, a man thrashing through the surf. Our bus fell silent as we watched this man. On and on he ran, into the surf, up the sand dunes, and across the stream. We watched until we were mesmerized. We watched until he obviously could no longer run—until he sat, a lone warrior, on the sand.

Someone, I do not remember who, said, "We need to talk with this man." The driver opened the door, and we all climbed out, clambered down the bank, and walked to where the runner sat.

"Who are you," someone asked.

"What are you doing here?" another asked.

A third man asked, "Why are you training in this harsh place?"

"I am training for the marathon," the runner said. "I drive a truck for a living and have difficulty finding a place to train in the city. I come here on my days off so that I can train as long and as hard as I wish." When asked how long he had been running, he answered, "Seriously, about 10 years." And when asked how long he had been coming here, he said, "Maybe 5 or 6 years."

I remember shaking my head and asking, "How long will you continue doing this?"

He looked at me and said, "Every year I have done a little better, and so long as I improve, I will train this way."

As we drove away, I heard them talking in the back of the bus. Even the great ones were impressed, and I believe that all of our lives were enriched for having met a lonesome marathoner that day!

My journal for March 18, 1967, reads "It is fairly clear today, though cool and windy . . . at 10:30 attended the technical meeting where the discussion was translated from English to French to Spanish . . . much confusion, some angry words?"

Doris and I boarded a bus to the race course at 12:45. It is beginning to rain. Doris is off jogging, and as I look around, I am amazed to discover that cross-country at this level is unlike anything that I have seen or imagined. There appear to be 2000–3000 spectators who have paid to sit in bleacher seats. There are cheerleaders, leading a riotous chant Belgie-Belgie-Roelants-Roelants (Gaston Roelants of Belgium earned a gold medal by winning the steeplechase in the 1964 Olympic Games). Doris is oblivious that all of this is happening around us—she just wants the race to start."

The men ran first, and I watched carefully as they negotiated the pasture—now free of cows. I soon discovered that the wet area was now a bog. Cows had wallowed there, and as the men ran through the bog, the mud sucked the shoes off several runners' feet. This was enough to convince me that we needed to use adhesive tape to securely fasten Doris' shoes before her race.

As noted earlier, our strategy was for Doris to follow—touch tight as we like to say—then pass in the bog and kick for the soccer field and finish line. As she had done in Vancouver some months earlier, Doris passed the lead runner much sooner than expected. An anonymous writer described what happened next. "There was no confusion over the identity of the probable winner once the race got under way. Doris Brown (world's fastest indoor mile at 4:40.4) lost no time in streaking to the front and after the first half mile only Rita Lincoln could even attempt to live with her. Even Rita, as tenacious as they come, had to give way at the end of the first mile (covered in 5:06 in spite of gale force wind), Mrs. Brown 40 yards up on Rita, with Joyce Smith a further 100 yards back in third place. By the finish, the 24 year old American who trains twice a day and covers up to 100 miles a week in training had extended her lead to 200 yards over Rita who just scraped home ahead of inspired Peggy Mullen."[13]

At the finish line, the BBC man once again put a microphone in Doris' face and now humbly asked, "How did you do it? How did you win?"

Doris responded by saying, "It was easier than I expected. I heard the other girls breathing heavily. I acted, I passed, and I won."

Later she said to me, "The real satisfaction in winning is, knowing that I ran just as hard and as fast as I could, that I proved something to myself."

This realization that she had the ability to compete when others might surrender to fatigue was a powerful lesson learned. Years later when responding to a question regarding her best race, Doris said, "My first world's championship in the cross-country in Wales in 1967—I was ahead entering the last half-mile and oh, so tired! I ran just as hard and as fast as I could. I won it, and this gave me some real satisfaction . . . a significant step in my development as a runner, and it was worthwhile." [14]

The post-meet celebration was a special time, with special people, albeit intimidating at first. Doris and I had never before been to such an event. We soon learned that when men and women discipline themselves for months, when they train to the point of physical pain day after day, they tend to play hard as well. We also were gratified by the obvious respect, almost a sense of awe that both the men and the women had for the little blonde girl from the USA. A runner from the South African team was especially impressed, saying again and again, "How do you run so many miles. I do not train that hard myself."

My favorite happening of the evening, other than having the Lord Mayor of Barry present Doris with her winning award, was watching Gaston Roelants dance with a half-filled wine bottle balanced on his head. He later gave Doris an autographed picture of himself and invited her to go dancing. On learning that Doris was married, Gaston graciously rescinded his offer, returned to the dance floor, and continued to dance with the bottle balanced on his head.

Before leaving the US for the International Cross-Country Meet, Doris and I had decided that when the race was over, we would travel to Paris for a few days of R and R. It would be time, we believed, to kick back, relax, and enjoy the sights of this great city. Upon arriving in Paris, we traveled by bus and taxi to the Rapp Hotel, highly recommended as economical and well situated to visit the Eiffel Tower. After check in, we had dinner, walked along the river, and returned to our hotel. Before going to our rooms, I suggested to Doris that she sleep in the following morning. "I'll get up early," I said, to look around, so that when you are awake, we can have breakfast and then take off for a leisurely day of sightseeing.

It was scarcely light when I stepped out of the hotel the following morning. Walking the few short blocks to the Eiffel Tower, I climbed to the lower viewing platform and stood marveling at the sight of Paris at dawn. There was a light fog rising from the parade ground to the east, and as I was looking that direction, I observed a runner. Though some distance away, the determined stride told me that it was my runner. Not mine in any possessive way, but mine in the way of mutual respect and association.

Doris, who had gotten up even earlier than I, was caught in her daily routine, running in the early morning light. It was a thing of beauty, flaxen hair dancing along new footprints on dew-covered grass in Parc Du Camp De Mars, obvious joy in every step. Tears filled my eyes. She was champion of the world. She was my champion. She was doing what had gotten her here, what would, perhaps, make a coach of me.

Honors for a Champion

We arrived home to discover that the Seattle Community now regarded Doris Brown as their "Woman of Achievement." Indeed, Doris' unexpected victory in the first International Cross-Country Championship for women, at Barry, Wales, on March 18, 1967, proved to be the defining event in a career that lasted more than a decade. A headline in the Everett Herald on 4/17/67 read, "GAL TRACK STAR TOUTED." The accompanying article stated that International track star Mrs. Doris Brown has been honored in a resolution approved unanimously by the Washington State House of Representatives. The headline and the resolution praised her "diligent training and hard work and her honored example for her pupils." (Appendix B)

Doris Brown receives her first place trophy from the mayor, Barry Wales

Coach and athelete discuss mile splits prior to the Barry event

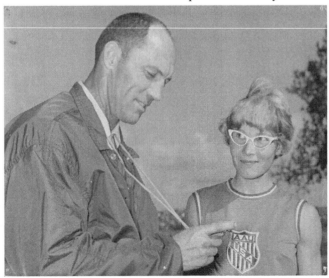

UNBELIEVABLE

I have been coaching a long time—57 years to be exact. When I look back to her decade, I do not now know how Doris (and others at her level of competition) was able to do, what she was able to do. It now seems unbelievable to me. The year of 1967 is a case in point. In her first race of the year (2/4/1967), she set a world indoor record in the 880y with a time of 2:08.5. Subsequent to the race, George Meyers, wrote "For the third straight year in succession, more than 10,000 addicts thronged the Coliseum. They were rewarded by a world-record run by the incredible Doris Brown in the half- mile and the third-fastest indoor two-mile in history-by Gerry Lingren." Meyers then noted that running without the help of someone "clinging to [her] heels, her achievement [was] one of the wonders of track history." [15]

Twelve days later, running in the Achilles Mile in Vancouver, B.C. she set a world indoor mark in the mile with the time of 4:40.4. Following a tense month of negotiations with the AAU and fund raising to subsidize the trip to Wales, Doris won her first of five international cross-country races, Barry, March 18, 1967. She trained and competed in local events through the months of April and May. On June 3rd Doris "set a blazing pace in winning the 880y at the Compton Relays—her time a personal best of 2:04.7—her closest pursuer, Charlotte Cooke was well back in 2:08.5."[16]

These meets were in some ways a preliminary for competitions yet to come. We now had to decide whether Doris would defend her NAAU title at 1500 meters, or run the 880y in hopes of qualifying for the U.S. team that would compete against the British Commonwealth and in the Pan American Games later in the summer. The 880y was loaded with longtime adversaries Manning, Cooke, Mulder, Francie Kraker and Jarvis Scott, but we believed that Doris could win and thus entered the shorter race.

The NAAU Championships were conducted in Santa Barbara, California, on July 1–2, 1967. The preliminary heats were hot, with Brown and Manning emerging as the runners to beat. In the championship race, both Manning and Brown broke the existing American record for 880 yards, running 2:03.6 and 2:03.9 respectively.

I had been selected, along with Chuck Coker, to coach the U.S. women's team and was elated when Doris qualified for the US International Team. We moved on to Los Angeles where we were billeted in housing on the campus of USC. As head coach, I assigned Chuck to the work with the field events, while I took responsibility for all running events, including the relays. One week after setting an American record at Santa Barbara, Madeline Manning won the 880y with an American record of 2:01.6. Judy Pollock of Australia was 2nd in 2:01.7 and Doris third in 2:05.5 (27.0–57.1–1:28.8–2:05.5).

With little more than time to fly home, wash, and repack, we flew off again to Minneapolis, Minnesota, to compete for a place on the US Pan American Team. In preliminary heats run on July 15, Doris and Madeline again proved to be the 800m runners to beat, though both showed signs of residual fatigue. On Sunday, July 16, Doris led for 799 2/3 meters, with Manning beating her to the tape in the time of 2:05.2–Doris' time 2:05.5. Jarvis Scott was third, posting a personal best time of 2:06.5.

We returned home, took three days of rest, and were back to two-a-day workouts in preparation for the Pan American Games to be held in Winnipeg, Canada. The 800m was contested on August 5, with Doris and Madeline again fighting for victory. In winning, Madeline Manning set a new meet record with a time of 2:02.3. Doris again was a close 2nd in 2:02.9 (28.5–60.0–1:30.6–2:02.9).

Five days later, on August10, a select group of American's competed against an all-star group in a meet billed as the USA vs Europe. The team from Europe easily defeated the fatigued Americans, though Manning and Brown placed first and third in a hotly contested 800m race (2:02.6 and 2:05.3).

The month of August was and is the first month of cross-country training for the Falcon Track Club. Following the USA vs Europe meet, Doris and I returned to Seattle— to rest and recover before returning to open spaces—rolling hills and wooded trails. Unfortunately, we were almost immediately pressured to have Doris participate in an international pre-Olympic meet in Mexico City. To my lasting regret, I did not stand firm in the face of pressure from the AAU, and I reluctantly agreed that she would compete in an 800m race against several of the top middle distance runners in the world.

Doris ran well enough in her preliminary heat (October 14) to face the likes of Mia Gomers (Holland) and Vera Nikolic (Yugoslavia) in the finals. In the kick to the finish (October 15), Doris was pushed, and in attempting to regain her balance, she re-injured a hamstring that had given her trouble since her college days. Doris finished 6th in 2:09.6 and flew directly to Seattle where she was evaluated by our team physician, Dr. Keith Peterson. Doris had a serious hamstring pull, was sent to physical therapy, and advised to lay off running for a month.

Like so many great athletes, Doris entered into a comprehensive rehabilitation program as if she were training for an Olympic event. Though she is not fond of water, she engaged in hours and hours of swimming, often in near freezing temperatures. Indeed, I have seen her climb out of

Green Lake in mid-winter as red as the proverbial lobster, often shaking so hard that she could not use a towel to dry off. After three weeks of intense rehab, Dr. Peterson agreed that she could resume jogging. One week before the PNAC Cross-Country Championships, Doris was permitted to run a modest, timed lap on our Green Lake course. She finished the 2.5-mile run pain free, though obviously lacking adequate aerobic fitness for national competition.

After careful consideration, we decided that Doris (who desperately wanted to defend her world title) would run in the PNAC Championship Cross-Country race. The PNAC race was contested over a familiar, 3000 meter, rolling course at Seattle's Woodland Park with teammates Vicki Foltz, Trina Hosmer, Nancy Main, Debbie Quatier and Linda Mayfield also competing. The plan was for Doris to tuck in behind a teammate, running for fitness rather than attempting to win. Vicki Foltz was winner in the excellent time of 9:49. Doris was a distant 2nd in 9:57, with Linda Mayfield 3rd in 9:59. Both Vicki and Linda went on to qualify for the 1968 International Cross-Country Team at the championship meet contested at Albuquerque, New Mexico. Doris, however, did not run again until after the Christmas season.

Other than the season-ending injury (actually, the torn hamstring had a long-term impact on Doris' running career), Doris had a strong season—albeit long and highly competitive. She ran ten so-called major races, four of which had qualifying heats. Unlike today when athletes at her level are fully subsidized, frequently travel first class, and are housed in top of the line hotels we had to raise all of our travel funds, fly coach and stay in economy facilities. This is not a complaint. It is, however, reality, and it raises the question—how good would Doris Brown have been if she had been able to run distances races more nearly matching her natural gifts? And, how good would she have been if she had had ready access to a trainer, a massage therapist, been able to train without pain and travel as if she were a world-class performer? How good indeed!

And, in my mind there is an equally important, corollary question. Why is it that women who do have the advantages referred to above, are not performing significantly better?

THE CIRCUITOUS ROAD
TO MEXICO CITY

In an interesting coincidence, a sports writer contacted me during the first week of December 1968. He was writing an article on "What track stars do in the off season?" With specific reference to Doris, I wanted to say some smart thing like active rest, but rather, had to inform him that Doris was injured and having a difficult time staying off her feet. I then related a recent incident that was later described in an article appearing in the "Wenatchee Daily World."

"Dr. Ken Foreman coach of the Falcon Track Club for which Mrs. Brown competes, said the petite school teacher aggravated a leg injury in competition at Mexico City and had to discontinue training . . . when I learned she was swimming in the lake I rushed over there and ordered her out, Foreman said. She wailed that she had to keep up her training some way, even if she couldn't run."[17]

Doris was, of course, stating a fact. 1968 was an Olympic year she was injured and frustrated and could not run. We had to find ways for her to stay fit, but swimming in freezing water was not the best choice. Since Doris enjoyed working in the weight room—the challenge of gymnastic type activities, particularly climbing ropes, doing chin ups, push ups, etc, we developed a so-called super circuit aimed at maintaining aerobic capacity and enhancing her overall fitness. In vintage Doris style, she attacked the circuit with near abandon, enhancing her chin up maximum to 28, her time up the 25' rope (without the use of her feet) to less than 15 seconds and her push up max to more than 100.

Doris also worked each day with a physical therapist who, helped to guide her in a progressive return to full activity. When she was pain free, she had to be restrained in her enthusiasm to "push it." (Her words) On January 20th our team physician gave us the green light to go for it! We thus accepted an invitation to run the mile in the Seattle Indoor to be held on February 4, intending to use that race as a marker of fitness. Doris won the mile, with teammate Vicki Foltz 2nd. Bob Payne described the race as follows; "Seattle's Doris Brown was predictably a brilliant winner of a 4:54.6 mile."[18] Suffice to say, she and I also were predictably pleased with her performance and the progress that she had made in spite of the injury that ended her 1967 season.

With two weeks of additional training, Doris won the mile run in the Achilles Federation Indoor Meet held in Vancouver, BC, in 4:51.1 (February 17) One-week later (February 23) Doris won the NAAU Indoor mile in the time of 4:50.2.

Subsequently, and without notifying coaches and athletes, the Women's Track and Field Committee of the Amateur Athletic Union selected a team of six women to represent the United States in the International Cross-Country Meet to be held in Blackburn, England on March 24, 1968. The six were Doris, FTC teammates Vicki Foltz and Linda Mayfield, Natalie Rocha, Lori Schutt and Cheryl Bridges. We learned about the team selection through a press release accrued by the clipping service at Seattle Pacific University. We also learned that the AAU would "handle all arrangements but the AAU budget did not permit underwriting transportation and living costs."

The press release and the statement about funding came as a slap in the face to Doris and me. In 1967 we had prevailed on our friend Royal Brougham, Sports Editor of the Seattle P-I, and Seattle's 101 Club to subsidize our trip to Barry, Wales. Her victory, we had believed, would provide the impetus for structured team selection and support by the AAU, but this obviously had not happened. "Handling all arrangements" at that point was a joke—notify the games committee that the US was sending a team, select a coach and then turn the athletes loose to fend for themselves.

The record will show that the US team was victorious in Blackburn scoring 19 points, England was 2nd with 20 and Scotland had 55 for 3rd. Doris won her second race over a rain swept, 3000 meter course in 15 minutes flat, Vicki was 2nd in 15:12, with Linda Mayfield the third American, placing 5th overall, her time 15:43. After winning, Doris was quoted, saying "It was a beautiful course. We really enjoyed it . . . my thanks are due to the students and faculty of my school back home who made it possible for me to come here."

The US Team victory was a shock to members of the British press who covered the meet. Mal Watman expressed surprise and near disbelief in the outcome of the International event saying "In its way, the American girls' triumph at Blackburn is as significant a happening as were the victories of Bob Schul and Billy Mills in the long distance track events at Tokyo (Olympic Games, 1964. My addition) As recently as two years ago anyone daring to predict that a US team could come over here and defeat the cream of England's cross–country runners would have risked being ridiculed. Last year, however, one marveled at Doris Brown at Barry and wondered how many more there were like her at home. Last Saturday the English girls found out."[19]

On this side of the Atlantic few people knew what the American women had accomplished, fewer yet were aware that members of the US Team had to raise money to represent their country in a prestigious international competition. One who did was Frank Eck, Sports Editor for AP News Features, who wrote "when a girl wants to run, she runs." How correct he was, girls/women on the 1968 International Cross-Country Team wanted to run enough to ask for help.

Doris went to her principle at Butler Jr. High School who contacted Rotary Clubs on her behalf. Here was a world champion having to beg for financial support to represent her country and defend her title.

Bill Schey wrote an informative article about the "25-year old track star, who attended high school at Peninsula in Purdy prior to attaining athletic fame as one of the nations finest distance runners . . . she'll be one of five U.S. females to take part in the second International Cross-Country Championship at Blackburn, England. Despite having won the meet last year, Mrs. Brown, as well as four other entries, must pay their own expense." [20]

Vicki Foltz took out a loan from a local bank into which supporters could deposit monetary gifts. The Lions Club of Cave Junction, Oregon and members of the Southern Oregon College football team, raised money for Linda Mayfield. Natalie Rocha was subsidized by her team, the Will's Spikettes who initiated a bottle collection drive on her behalf. Lori Schutt received support from students and faculty at the University of Illinois. Cheryl Bridges, who planned to be married soon after returning to the United States, included a note with her wedding announcements regarding her need for financial assistance

After all the hassle to raise money, travel and competition, we were ready for cross-country to be over. Thus upon returning home we took a brief rest before moving forward with preparations for the road to the Olympic Games. Initially cautious, Doris ran only two races during May, a 4:43.5 1500 meters as part of a fund raiser for a Falcon Track Club team mate who wanted to go to college. And the Oregon AAU Championships (May 28) where she won the mile on the rain swept track in the time of 4:51.6 (70–2:26–3:40–4:51.6). Doris completed a noteworthy double on June 10 and 11, winning an 800 meter race in Los Angeles—2:05.7 on the 10th and winning the PNAAU mile championships in

Seattle—4:42.2 on the 11th. Our focus now turned to international competition, with races scheduled in both London and Dublin—arranged and subsidized by Billy Morton, an Irish meet promoter. We were particularly anxious to have Doris run at London's Crystal Palace as it would give her the opportunity to compete with top Olympic contenders from Europe.

One week prior to the scheduled date for Doris to fly to England we were informed by Ollan Cassell, executive director of the AAU that Doris could not compete in Europe without an AAU sanction . . . she could not travel without an officially assigned chaperone and she could not accept money from Billy Morton. We were stunned, first the funding fiasco where the US international cross-country team was concerned, and now this. The following article appearing in the Seattle P-I tells the rest of the story.

$700 Worth of Red Tape

"You say you're tired of reading about the Great Alphabet War between the AAU, the NCAA, the USTFF and the USOC? Then scroonch over on your love seat there, Sidney. You've got company.

Let's talk about Doris Brown, instead. For one thing, she's prettier than Avery Brundage. For another, she can run faster than Ollan Cassell. In fact, she is one of the top women runners in the United States and a definite contender for Olympic laurels.

So Doris Brown should receive all the help and encouragement an organization like the AAU can provide. Shouldn't she? In theory, yes. In practice? Well, you decide.

Three or four months ago Doris received an invitation to compete in a mile race scheduled in Dublin, Ireland. Her coach, Ken Foreman, thought that race and a couple of others the same week in England, would greatly assist Doris in her preparation for the U.S. Olympic Trials.

The promoter of the Dublin track meet, Billy Morton, sent a letter to the AAU requesting a travel permit for Doris. And he agreed to pay her travel expenses in the meet. Thus, preparations for her tour appeared to be completed, a good three months in advance.

Then just a few days ago the AAU, through Ollan Cassell, suddenly declared Doris could make the trip to London only if she had a chaperone. Now Doris is a schoolteacher, 25 years old and happily married. She has taken similar trips in the past with AAU sanction and without a chaperone, and has managed to avoid the clutches of the white slavers.

But Cassell said unless an authorized chaperone accompanied her this time, she would be unable to make the trip. Don Brown, her husband, would not fit the definition of an authorized chaperone. An authorized chaperone is an AAU official, probably living in New York, who wouldn't mind taking an expense paid trip to Ireland this summer.

Little Additional Expense

Anyway, Cassell instructed Doris to Demand that the Dublin Promoter, Billy Morton, provide additional expense money for a chaperone. Doris refused because the demand was unrealistic and unfair. But she still wanted to compete in the three meets in Ireland and England.

"What would happen if I received no expense money from Billy Morton" Doris finally asked the AAU. "What would happen if I paid my own way to Ireland?"

The AAU officials hemmed and hawed, and finally said that would be satisfactory. If Doris paid her own way to Ireland, the AAU would allow her to travel without a chaperone.

So that is what she did. Doris and her husband also a Seattle school teacher, didn't have enough saving to pay for the trip. So they borrowed the money. They went $700 in debt so that she could make the trip to Dublin, and could gain some added racing experience that could well help her win a gold or silver or bronze medal for this country at the Olympics this fall.

If you are mystified by the edicts of the AAU, you needn't be. As anybody familiar with international competition can tell you, some AAU officials don't much care for Billy Morton of Dublin. And quite often they'll attempt to make if difficult for U.S. athletes to compete in their meets.

Never Mind the Consequences

In other words, they'll sometimes punish a kid like Doris Brown, so that they can score a minor point in their petty war with a Dublin Promoter.

Now this bears no relation to the current war between the AAU and the NCAA, except for this:

It does point up how a few pompous officials can lose sight of the ultimate aims of athletics . . . to make it as easy as possible for athletes, of all countries to meet as equals on the field of sport.

If you remain mystified by the plight of hapless pawns like Doris Brown, then you simply never encountered a stuffed shirt . . . a shirt stuffed with official ribbons, lofty titles, misused power and petty jealousies

As long as such stuffed shirts occupy seats of command, they'll continue to wage war. And the only casualties will be the athletes they claim they're trying to protect."[21]

After much soul searching, we agreed that Doris would run in England and Ireland as previously planned. Her first race was (July 20) at London's Crystal Palace, where she ran against several of the top middle distance runners in Europe. At the finish of this epic race, she had run the fastest 800 meters that she would ever run. Vera Nikolic set a new world record in the time of 2:00.5. Doris ran 2:02.2 (60.7–2:02.2), placing 3rd behind Lillian Board of England. Doris remembers the London experience as "a super couple of days . . .

spending time with the absolute best runners in the world."

If life permitted second-guessing, we likely would not have gone to England and Ireland to run in such heady competition so early in the season. But you only get one chance to make such decisions—we were learning. As strange as that may seem now, it is a fact that in 1968 (other than the tragic women's 800 meter race during the 1928 Olympic Games at Amsterdam) girls and women had only been running 880y/800 meters for eight years. When I accompanied Marcia Cosgrove to the Olympic Trials in 1956, the longest race for women was the 220y. Too, there were fewer than a dozen, high quality middle distance runners in the US in 1968, and probably not more than 30 in the entire world. To make things worse, as an Eastern Block coach once said to me "your problem in American is that you do not share information with each other." He was correct, those of us who were fortunate enough to be working with talented female athletes were, in a sense, an experiment of one, toiling alone in the trenches, we learned, or we failed, as we went along.

Los Alamos—More than the Atomic City

The Olympic stadium at Mexico City stands at more than 5000' above sea level. We were learning, but knew enough to understand that middle distance runners, competing at that altitude, needed to be acclimated, to develop an adaptive response to elevation. To prepare for competition in Mexico City, our men trained at Truckee, then a small town on the California-Nevada border. The women, having held their 1967 Heptathlon Championships at Los Alamos, NM, chose to establish their high elevation training camp in this Atomic City. The first women to train at Los Alamos were members of the Falcon Track Club, i.e., Doris, Vicki Foltz, Judy Oliver and Patty Engberg. The ladies stayed with local families, followed schedules I had developed for training at 6500'and were assisted in timing and record keeping by engineers from the Los Alamos Laboratory.

During their first stay at Los Alamos Doris and I communicated daily and exchanged detailed letters at the end of each week. In her first letter, Doris wrote "things are going well here for all of us," she then noted that "yesterday was better than you asked, even. We did the entire workout. Vicki was just a little behind me—Doris went on to say, "It wasn't easy but it's the first one I could do. I've been getting cramps in my legs, but each day I get a little further before they strike—like the last interval today" She ended this letter with a comment about the good will of the people of Los Alamos. "Everyone seems to have a stop watch here . . . it is so easy to be timed in all of our workouts."

(Remember, Los Alamos, all of those scientific types, they live by facts, like to weigh and measure things? Dr. Harmon Brown and I later utilized this scientific expertise while working with the women's Olympic team)

Two weeks into her first stay at Los Alamos Doris completed a Monday workout, running 15 x 220y, all under 32 seconds. Recovery was a 220y jog. On Tuesday of that week she ran 3 x 440y in 60–61.8–60.4, with a 440y jog recovery. She wrote that "her legs cramped . . . had to quit . . . would have had trouble doing anymore." Then she asked, "next time would 4 be enough?" It certainly was enough!

After completing three weeks of high elevation training our ladies returned to Seattle, rested for two days and we were on the road to Aurora, Colorado host city for the women's NAAU Championship meet. With seven entries in the championships and limited financial resources, we were forced to drive from Seattle to Colorado. We arrived in a rainstorm trained in a rainstorm and competed on a rain soaked dirt track.

On the evening of August 18 Doris won the 800m in 2:05.1, Francie Kraker was 2nd in 2:07.8 and Madeline Manning 3rd in 2:07.6 (Splits 62.5–2:05.1). The following morning we turned our automobiles to the west, headed over the Rockies', then across desert country to the city of Walnut, California, site of the Olympic Trials for women. We arrived, fatigued from the heat and hours of sitting, but excited, believing that Doris was a strong contender for a place on the Olympic Team.

The Olympic Trials for women were scheduled for Saturday and Sunday, August 24–25. Upon arriving at Mt. San Antonio's Memorial Stadium we were shocked to discover that semi-finals and finals in the 800m were scheduled for the same night—a lesser shock, yet one giving us concern was learning that three of the four fastest 800m runners in the country were loaded into the second semi-final heat; Doris Brown, Jarvis Scott and Francie Kraker. Manning, running in the first semi-final heat, had only our Vicki Foltz with whom to contend. Manning easily won her heat as expected. Doris was a winner as well, with Scott and Kraker running 2nd and 3rd.

The eight finalists had less than three hours to rest and recover. Our strategy was for Doris to go out fast to take the kick out of Manning and Scott both sub 53-second quarter milers. The strategy worked, almost as Doris and Madeline ran a dead heat, finishing in 2:03.0, with Jarvis 3rd in 2:04.5. (Doris' splits were 28–59.5–2:03). Our emotions were legion, satisfaction, excitement, but mostly we were overcome with great relief. It had been a tough month, all of us were tired, "oh so tired" we just wanted to get home and rest.

My Phone was Ringing

Two more days of driving and when I walked into my house in Seattle the phone was ringing—the caller was Marilyn West, manager of the women's Olympic Team. Marilyn informed me that neither, Alex Ferenczy or Conrad Ford Olympic team coaches could get off work and asked, "How soon can you get to Los Alamos and open the high elevation training camp." I responded saying, "give me two days to wash my clothes, repack and I will head for the hills."

Upon arriving in Los Alamos I contacted Mr. Roy Rider, fire control captain for the atomic laboratory, host to our Falcon Ladies earlier in the summer. Roy introduced me to a group of top school administrators with whom I negotiated for use of the High School facilities and equipment. School personnel were super, giving us freedom to use high school facilities and equipment as often as we wished. While I was securing the training site, Marilyn arranged for housing and meals at the Los Alamos Inn. The following day we conducted our first scheduled training session with five athletes in attendance, Doris, Madeline Manning, Francie Kraker, Lois Drinkwater and Nancy Shafer.

My entry the first night at Los Alamos was the first of what was to become a detailed journal of the Los Alamos experience. I wrote, "what a day . . . it has been a peak experience as described by Abraham Maslow . . . out of the ordinary . . . leaving one in awe, it humbles, it elevates . . . a life changing reality that like joy just happens?" My sense of purpose and contentment was difficult to describe.

Never before, nor since, have I been in a situation so rich with the beauty of friendships, so free from the press of extraneous demand and so full of potential for achieving sought after goals. Watching Doris, Madeline, Francie, Lois and Nancy warm up that first day was a coaches' dream come true. Seeing them run together was pure symphony. I loved it! I love it still!

Dr. Harmon Brown arrived with a large group of athletes on the evening of September 5th, and the following day we initiated two-a-day training sessions. The morning session was scheduled for 7:00 am. Two days a week we transported the athletes to a private cattle ranch situated above 8000'. There they could run with abandon on miles and miles of flat, dirt roads. On alternate days the morning runs were conducted at the Los Alamos country club where Dr. Brown monitored pulse rates while I supervised technical aspects of specific event preparation. The afternoon sessions were conducted on the high school track—with a staggered time schedule for sprints-hurdles, jumps and throws. Harmon and I were on the track most days from 1:00 pm to about 5:00 pm.

Shortly after we arrived in Los Alamos, Dr. Brown began looking for a place where our throwers could lift. Strength training for females was not highly popular at that time and he did not find an adequate venue for such activity. To solve the problem, he and I assembled a makeshift, strength training facility under the high school bleachers, and that became a regular evening activity.

Perhaps the thing that surprised me most about the Los Alamos experience is that a majority of the ladies arrived without daily training schedules. Most did not even have the rudiments of a plan. When the Pan American team trained at Los Alamos in 1975, Jan Merrill and Cindy Bremser gave me detailed training schedules and their coaches were in contact with me on a daily basis. But not so in 1968 when Harmon and I met with individual members of the Olympic team to develop an appropriate training strategy. The first 10-day cycle appears in Appendix C.

In retrospect, it was of particular interest to Dr. Brown and me that Madeline Manning, winner of the gold medal at Mexico City, "credits her conditioning to time spent training at Los Alamos." [22] A great deal has been written about the men's high elevation experience at Truckee however the Los Alamos experience seems to have been forgotten.

There were other positive consequences of the Los Alamos experience. Perhaps the most important of these was watching a disparate group of individuals come together as a team. This likely occurred as a result of activities off the track, as well as during training sessions on the track. Two such experiences that Harmon and I will long remember were a hunt for arrow heads in the Vaya Grande and the search for cave dwellings in Bandelier National Monument. Willie White and Mamie "Sticks" Rallins joined Harmon and me as we looked for arrow heads, though they later admitted that they "thought we were nuts for scratching away at the ground for something that they were not certain even existed." At Bandelier, Marin Seidler led as she and her teammates deftly scaled the red rock walls. They giggled like children while searching for the home of the Anasazi.

One Saturday evening we received word that Joe Robichaux had shipped several hundred ice cream bars to be shared with the "folk at Los Alamos." Harmon and I were dispatched to the Santa Fe airport to rescue the precious cargo, only to learn that the aircraft had flown on to Albuquerque. When the station agent in Santa Fe called his counter part at Albuquerque, he was told where we could put the sticky mess.

In addition to enjoying a positive training experience, our time at Los Alamos provided valuable information about world class, female athletes. Utilizing facilities at the Atomic Energy Laboratory, Dr. Brown and I were afforded the opportunity to accrue highly accurate measures of body density for a very select population of women. This information added to our emerging understanding of amenorrhea, a condition having far reaching implications for girls and women. We also noted that an initial physiological response to intense training at elevations above 6000', was a diminished hematocrit, i.e., a decrement in the bloods capacity to carry oxygen to working muscles and that positive changes, or an elevated hematocrit did not began to occur until the end of 3–4 weeks of such training. This finding seemed to provide evidence that short-term training at elevation had little, positive effect, on the trainee.

And while sprinters did not experience a decrement in

performance, middle distance runners did, almost incrementally according to the distance run. Time trials conducted at Los Alamos revealed that Doris' best marks were affected as follows:

Best 440y at sea level 55.3. . . . .best at altitude 56.4
Best mile at sea level 4:42.2. . . .best at altitude 4:52

Like Falling off a Cliff

Los Alamos is situated on a plateau, nearly surrounded by mountains—business center to the east—atomic energy Labs scattered through pine trees to the west. In 1968 there was one short airstrip to serve a steady flow of scientists and visitors. The airstrip started at the edge of the plateau and continued up hill to its terminus hard against the community of homes and business. Commuter aircraft served the community with several flights each day. Landing was not so bad but the take off was comparable to falling off a cliff—sheer terror as the aircraft roared down hill, flew off the end of the runway and dropped out of sight.

What a way to end our stay at Los Alamos, though perhaps symbolic of what lay ahead. After all the turmoil in Mexico City, housing conflicts, inadequate training venues, the black athlete boycott, most would say the experience was not so bad, others would admit to a sense of sheer terror when entering the Olympic stadium, and regrettably when it was all over some just dropped out of sight.

Doris Qualifies for Finals—Does Not Medal

I returned to Seattle after leaving Los Alamos, unpacked, washed clothing, repacked and in less than 24 hours was on my way to Mexico. This time my wife, 12-year-old son and I were driving—headed for the city of Cuernavaca where I had contracted to serve as tour guide for a group of track and field enthusiasts. My first act upon arriving in Cuernavaca was to contact Doris, who assured me that she was well and anxious to run. We visited the Olympic Village the following day, attended a training session and met with acquaintances and friends in and about the track. One of those acquaintances made an impression on my son that we both remember to this day.

We were watching the throwers workout, when Ed Burke turned and said "hello" to us. He then spoke directly to Tim, asking how he was and if he was enjoying himself here in Mexico? It wasn't so much what he asked, as the manner in which he spoke to this 12 year old boy. When Tim describes the incident he says, "he (Ed Burke) made me feel important, and that, coming from an Olympic Athlete, made a powerful impact on my life."

On October 17, after more than 10 months of preparation Doris placed 2nd in her preliminary heat of the 800m. Her time, 2:09.6 was indicative that hers' was a so-called-kickers race. We determined that Doris would front run in her semi final heat to take the kick out of her opponents, back off at the finish if she had a comfortable lead—she ran 2:05.2, placing 2nd again.

Finals for the women's 800 meter race were held on October 20. Vera Nikolic, world record holder had dropped out of competition for "personal reasons" adding to our expectation that if Doris ran her race, she would place in the top three finishers. But it was not to be. Running in 4th place coming into the final straightway, "ready to make her move . . . she glanced around for racing room . . . was jostled, stumbled and instead of speeding up, began slowly to fall back."[23] Manning sprinted to a new world and Olympic record in 2:00.9, with Ilona Silai 2nd in 2:02.5, and Mia Gommers 3rd in 2:02.8. Doris was 5th with the time of 2:03.9

After the Olympics were over, five American athletes were invited to run in Santiago, Chile. In competition that included teammate, Francie Kraker, Doris won both the 400m and 800m events. Her time in the 800m was 2:05.6.

When asked about the South American trip, Pat Van Wolvelaere expressed the sentiment of the American visitors saying, "Marvelous" . . . it was a very nice trip."

1968 was a testimonial to the commitment, courage and competitive spirit of Doris Brown. Beginning with a 4:54.6 indoor mile on February 4—a 2nd victory in International Cross-County competition in March—a personal best of 2:02.2 in the 800 meters in July—victory at 800 meters at the NAAU Championship meet during August—a dead heat finish running a 2:03.0. 800m at the Olympic trials - a 4:52.0 mile at 7000' elevation in September—two 2nds and a 5th place finish in the Olympic trials and finals—two victories in an added International meet in October—ending with a 15:08.7 victory in a 2.9 mile cross-country race on December 14th it had been a very long, competitive season. It was time to rest.

BEING THE BEST IS NEVER EASY

1968 had been a long, hectic, exciting and challenging year for Doris and me. As we looked ahead to 1969 we made the decision to limit competition on the track and focus primarily on cross-country. One reason for our decision was Doris' proclivity toward soft tissue injury. Another was the fact that cross-country was becoming a popular club sport in America—with a dramatic increase in both the number and the quality of participating runners. It was becoming more and more obvious that if Doris was to continue to be the best cross-country runner in the world we had to give greater attention to off track training.

Because the Canadians had (though initially with reluctance) been first to give Doris the opportunity to compete at an international level we agreed to run one indoor race prior to the International Cross-Country event. The indoor 800m, February 8, an added attraction for British Columbia track and field fans to watch their American hero race, was won by Doris in the now pedestrian time of 2:10.2. With her weekly mileage at 80, we continued working at volume rather than intensity—changing to race tempo the first week of March.

In this third year of International competition the AAU provided some financial assistance for the US team. The Championship event was held in Clydebank, Scotland on March 22, 1969. Doris recalls a tough race on a golf course with steep hills and sand traps with no place that was easy to run. Smiling, she said after the race "it was my kind of course . . . maybe that is why I won." Her time for 4000m on a cold and ugly day was 14:46, with Maureen Dickson, also of the USA a close 2nd in 14:51. Falcon Track Club teammates Vicki Foltz and Judy Oliver were 16th and 17th respectively.

In keeping with our plan to limit competition on the track Doris did not run again until May 3rd—winning the 880y in a local meet in 2:10.9. Her next serious race (June 3) was 800m in the Compton-Coliseum Relays, where she placed 2nd to Madeline Manning with a time of 2:07.4. Doris returned to Seattle with a sore hamstring, our team physician recommended rest and rehabilitation for two weeks after which she could return to easy running.

Thus with limited running and a focus on pace training, we traveled to Dayton, Ohio for the NAAU meet held on July 5–6, 1969. Reminiscing about her long running career, Doris remembers the Dayton meet as a time when "I limped through finals, managing to win the 1500m in something like 4:30." Actually her time was 4:27.3. Not bad for a "wounded warrior."

We returned to Seattle with intent to prepare prudently for the US Team tour of Europe. With alternate days of off track fun running, Doris completed a tough workout on July 18, running repeat 880s in 2:15.3–2:15.4, with a 10 minute jog recovery. She felt strong and was excited to run in Europe where she posted times of 4:17.0, 4:18.6 and 4:18.5 (1500m) in Stuttgart, Augsburg and London. Returning home, Doris again took time for fun running before final preparation for the Pacific Conference Games scheduled for Tokyo on September 27–28, 1969. Her final training session prior to leaving for Japan was a 3 x 300m step down with a 100m, walk recovery. Doris ran 45–44–43, saying, "coach I believe I am ready." In her final appearance on the track in the 1969 season, Doris was 2nd in the 800m in Tokyo, 2:05.4, and first in the 1500m, 4:19.9.

The transition from track to the wooded trails was a joy for Doris as she was a cross-country runner at heart. She looked forward to running again without the constraint of ovals and curbs. We started with several days of active rest, a hike at the Foltz farm, scenic jogging on trails in Rainier National Park, fun running among the falling leaves of the University of Washington arboretum gradually increasing volume and intensity. On November 8 we conducted our first test run, a fast, flat 2 miler at Green Lake in which Doris posted a lifetime best of 10:05.

The following week our Falcon Track Club competed in the Canadian National Cross-Country Championships over a modestly difficult 4000m course. Doris won, setting a course record of 14:28, teammate Vicki Foltz 2nd.

As noted earlier, by 1969 cross-country was enjoying wide interest and popularity in the United States. With little athletic activity in schools and colleges, club teams dominated the competitive scene for girls and women. The most competitive of these were Will's Spikettes, San Jose Cindergals, Wolverine Parkettes, Duke City Dashers, Long Beach Comets, Oregon Track Club, Phoenix Fliers and the Falcon Track Club. Each team boasted one or more outstanding runners, four of whom were undefeated going into the 1969 championship event—Francie Larrieu-San Jose, Cheryl Bridges-Parkettes, Debbie Roth-Oregon and Doris Brown-Falcons.

The field of potential winners was so deep that Vince Reel wrote, "In addition to the undefeated runners, seven other top ranked athletes will force the pace as the runners clash to determine not only the US champion, but to select the six runners for the USA team at the World Championships in March."[24] We were quite aware that Doris would have to run the race of her life to defeat the quality field of entries in the championship meet. We also knew from having visited the racecourse that long grass would take its toll on those not prepared for an unforgiving running surface. Thus it was that we returned to the tide flats of Puget Sound to train in sand in preparation for Inglewood's La Cienega

Park (Southern California).

In what some described as the toughest field ever assembled for a U.S. cross-country championships, Doris led from the start, running over a soft, undulating course she stretched her lead into an amazing 18 second victory over teammate Vicki Foltz , Cheryl Bridges, Francie Larrieu, Pam Bagian and Pat Cole.

Our training strategy for the year paid off—focusing on volume, with limited speed training had resulted in 1969 being a huge success.

A TIME FOR CHANGE

S ome things just happen at the wrong time—one was our selection process for the US International cross-country team. The years 1969–1970 were a poignant reminder of this reality. The group of runners, characterized by Vince Reel "as the toughest field ever assembled" (1969 NAAU Cross-Country Championships) were described as "pathetic" at the 1970 International Cross-Country Championships.

I knew all members of our US team personally and did not then, and do not now, believe they deserved the harsh criticism they received. It was our selection system that was pathetic, not the young women who competed for the US team. We somehow expected our runners to peak in November for our National Championship meet, maintain their high level of fitness through the winter and be ready to compete in the International meet in March. This surely was a kind of madness, especially when most of our top runners also participated in indoor track and field.

But this is getting ahead of the story. Doris was able to maintain her competitive edge because she loved to run, was a committed cross-country runner. She also had the advantage of mild winters, great places to train and teammates Vicki Foltz and Trina Hosmer a world-class cross-country skier, with whom to train. Following a brief period of active rest subsequent to the NAAU cross-country meet, Doris and Trina skied (cross-country) every weekend from December to February. (Nordic skiers, we now know, have the highest recorded V02 max measures of any group of athletes)

With limited running training, Doris posted a time of 2:12.7 on January 10, 1970. The following weekend she ran in the Portland Indoor, where she won the invitational mile in 4:46.0 (68.2–2:22–3:34–4:46.0). We continued to train off the track, except for two days of pace work prior to the Seattle Indoor scheduled for February 7, 1970. Well aware of the risk of being overly optimistic, we laid out a race plan that, if realistic, would be on world record pace. (67–2:17–3:28-go for it!)

On Sunday, February 8 a head line in the Seattle Times read, "Doris' Plan Proves Perfect." Doris won her race, setting a world indoor record for 1500m in 4:21.1. (67.2–2:17.3–17.3–3:30–4:21.1). George Meyers described the world record run as an "outstanding performance . . . Doris went to the lead from the start and steadily pulled away . . . the race was set up as a duel between Doris and Francie Larrieu . . . the pair share the American outdoor record for the 1,500m of 4:16.8. Miss Larrieu, 4:35.5, finished a distant second." Doris received a unanimous vote as "The Outstanding Athlete of the Meet."[25]

Doris and Francie met again the following week in the Times Indoor Games at the Los Angeles Arena. (February 13) A summary report of the meet noted that "Doris Brown of Seattle continued to prove her versatile ability at distance running by winning the women's 880y in a meet- record time of 2:09.5. She beat Francie Larrieu of San Jose by 6 seconds. A week ago in Seattle Doris set a world indoor record for 1,500 meters."[26]

Some months earlier we had agreed that Doris would run a race in Canada during the 1970 indoor season. It was with reluctance that we honored the agreement, having Doris run in Regina, Saskatchewan on (February 21), just one month before the 4th International Cross-Country Championships scheduled for Fredrick, Maryland on March 22. Doris won her race, 800 meters in 2:07.3.

Jack Griffin, coach of the Fredrick Track Club, a pioneer in track and field and cross-country for girls and women, was a driving force behind the sponsorship of several championship events in his hometown. The first International Cross-Country Championships meet contested in the United States was held in Fredrick as a consequence of his stature in the world of athletics. And, as always had been true, the citizens of this host city went out of their way to make the event a positive experience for all of the participants.

The race was contested on a wet, soggy, albeit an otherwise well-groomed, modestly difficult course. Cross-country buffs considered the race an even test between the experienced Brits and the Americans, boasting veteran runners Doris Brown, Cheryl Bridges, Pat Cole . . . and hard charging Francie Larrieu and Pam Bagian, (Shirley Springer was a replacement for injured veteran Vicki Foltz), but it was not to be. In his report to the AAU, Dick Beyst, coach for the US Team stated, "our girls did not appear prepared." He also described all members of the team except Doris, "as pathetic." [27]

Doris won her fourth consecutive title over the 2.5-mile course in the time of 15:04.4, a 7-second margin of victory over runner-up Rita Ridley of England.

An article appearing under the headline "DORIS BROWN CONTINUES MASTERY IN HARRIER EVENT" described Doris' victory as "a sudden surge to the front and then a stretch run that wiped out all doubt about the outcome . . . she challenged on the first-hill climb, yielded the lead for a while in the middle and then won it with a strong surge on the final up-hill climb that carried her well ahead of the field." [28]

The team scores were England 18, USA 46, Eire 48, Canada 58, Scotland 68, and Wales 87. Subsequent to our qualifying meet, which was held nearly four months earlier, it appeared that the US team would be hard to beat. It was now obvious to almost everyone that our system was broke; it needed to be fixed.

Returning to Seattle, Doris continued with easy fun running for several days before shifting attention to the forthcoming track and field season. With a focus on what I choose to call "strong-side training," maximizing natural gifts, aerobic capacity, and a disciplined work ethic for Doris, we prepared for the first competitive 3000m of Doris' running career. On April 25, four weeks after winning the Fredrick meet, Doris set a world record for 3000m (April 25) in 9:44.6.

Our training strategy was working as Doris ran a 4:47 mile on a wet and windy day in mid-May, and with 90 minutes of rest, she returned to the track to run 2:12.1 for 800m (68–2:24–3:37–4:47//63.5–2:12.1). The following week (May 30) Doris completed a particularly strong workout running 1320 yards in 3:28.6 (67.5–2:19–3:28.6), followed by thirty minutes of jogging before running 600 yards in 1:22.3 (59.2–1:22.3).

On June 13, Doris again ran two strong races, winning the mile in 4:45 (68–2:193.-3:33–4:45) and 800m in 2:06.0 (63–2:06.0). Unfortunately, her hamstrings were sore the following day, and we had to back off in our preparation for the National AAU meet scheduled for July 4 and 5. And that is another story!

The Falcon Track Club had a number of national-caliber athletes during the late '60s and early '70s. These included Lynette Matthews, shot and discus, as well as distance runners Trina Hosmer, Vicki Foltz, Judy Smith, Laurel Miller, Linda Mayfield, and Nancy Main. (Both Lynette and Laurel started competing while Doris was their Jr. high school coach) All were entered in the NAAU Meet—Lynette, first to compete, placed 3rd in the shot with a put of 48' 10 ½."

Later in the day Doris, Trina, Laurel, and Nancy ran in preliminary heats for the 1500m. Doris, Nancy, and Trina qualified for finals—Doris winning her heat in the modest time of 4:37.9. The three Falcon TC runners were scheduled to meet Francie Larrieu in the championship race the following day. When Francie was ready to race she was capable of setting a fast pace and holding on or following and kicking with the best. We believed that with Doris at less than her best, she needed to control the pace and hope to meet Francies' challenge at the end. Our strategy seemed to be working until Francie blew by to win; Doris was 2nd (67.2–2:18.2–3:29.4–4:24.30), and Trina was 3rd (4:29.2).

We returned to Seattle determined that Doris would rest, which to Doris was understood as cut back a little, do not run 10 miles to school at 5:30 A.M., stay off the track for a few days, and swim (which she hated because she was a sinker—almost no fat, just muscle, viscera, and bone). She did, however, recognize that ten years of hard training were taking their toll, and she needed a modest change of pace.

My records show that during September and October Doris trained primarily in places that she most enjoyed: the University of Washington Arboretum, along the shores of Lake Washington, the fields and woods of Camp Casey (Seattle Pacific University field station), the forest surrounding the Foltz home, and one trip to the high trails of Mt. Rainier National Park. Doris' first real competitive event in the fall of 1970 was a mid-November, 2-mile race that she won in 10:50.

Her second race was the NAAU Cross-Country Championships contested in St. Louis, Missouri, November 28. More than 90 runners reported for the start, including such veteran international competitors as Doris, Vicki Foltz, Cheryl Bridges, Maria Stearns, Judy Smith, Debbie Heald, Shirley Springer, and Francie Larrieu. "The race was hotly contested; Doris striding into the lead, followed by Beth Bonner over a soft, rain soaked course. In the end, the results were largely as expected; two defending champions, Doris Brown and the Wolverine Track Club, successfully repeating their 1969 triumphs as they won the National AAU cross-country titles . . . Wolverines 39, FTC 40."[29]

Doris hamstrings were tender after the St. Louis race so we adopted a cautions approach to training. Our long term goal was winning the International Cross-Country Championships scheduled for San Sebastian, Spain the following March. On December 18, 1970, Doris won a low-key race over a tough 3-mile course in Seattle's Lower Woodland Park with a time of 17:40. She ended the year, running in the Knights of Columbus Indoor meet, in Saskatchewan, Canada, on (December 29/30). Her winning times were 2:08.5 (61.8–2:08.5) for 800m, and 4:23.7 for 1500m.

It was time to go cross-country skiing again.

Man of the Year in Sports

On January 5, 1971, the front-page headline in the Seattle Post Intelligencer read, "Doris Brown Named P-Is MAN OF THE YEAR IN SPORTS." During her response to this prestigious award Doris was asked about her dedication to her sport. She responded saying, "Running is the most important aspect of my life at present." As I look back now I am certain that one of Doris' strengths as a competitive runner was her ability to compartmentalize, to focus on what was important to her, at the exclusion of other things. That ability likely was the primary reason why 1971 was a highlight year in her remarkable running career. (After reading a draft copy of this manuscript Doris sent me a note in which she wrote, "My faith was and is the most important aspect of my life." When answering the question about dedication I was referring to temporal things like work, study, play, etc.)

As Doris and I contemplated the year ahead, we were aware of the complexity of the challenge, initially having to choose between running on the track or over the wooded trail. We decided to emphasize the wooded trail with four exceptions, two indoor meets in January—two in February—a change of pace, a faster tempo, with the primary emphasis, however, on cross-country.

On January 10 Doris ran a 2:12.7 880y on a flat, indoor track. (31.5–64–1:38.5–2:12.7). With two weeks of additional training, she ran the mile at the Oregon Indoor (January 30). Her winning time was 4:45.6. In preparation for the Seattle Indoor (February 6), Doris had two days of pace training and a rest day prior to competition. She wowed the crowd with a strong 800m (2:07.3). On February 26, Doris defended her indoor title, winning the mile at the NAAU Championships in New York City. Her winning time, a modest 4:47.3, was, however, a tough challenge. Struck by a photographer's camera on lap 1 and held back by a crowded track, she had to work for her victory.

Returning to Seattle, we focused specifically on anticipated race conditions for the forthcoming International Cross-Country Championships. This included running many tempo miles on soft, grass surfaces. A 7:45.6, 1.5 time trial on a wet, cold course, 15 days prior to the International event indicated readiness. As it turned out, conditions for the time trial proved to be similar to the weather on race day in San Sebastian, Spain.

In 1971, while serving as Chairman of Women's Long Distance Running, I was selected by the AAU's International committee to be team leader for the US women's cross-country team. With limited progress in accruing support for our women through the national governing body, it continued to be a responsibility of the team leader and team personnel to raise their own travel funds. As committee chairman, it also was my responsibility to arrange for team travel, communicate with the host nation, secure housing, complete entry forms etc. Needless to say, my plate was full.

Members of the US Team quite literally came from all across the nation: New England to San Francisco to Seattle—from cities between. To accrue the lowest possible airfare for each participant, arrangements were made to send two groups to Madrid, with team manager Juner Bellew accompanying one group out of NY, the other group flying from Seattle with me. Ollan Cassell, Executive Director of the AAU suggested that "each individual retain funds raised in the different communities and purchase flight tickets in accordance with prearranged schedule . . . this I feel will also give the local community more prestige since the tickets may be purchased by a local agent."[30] Big deal, we raise the funds and now we have permission as to how they will be used. Typical AAU double talk!

The Seattle group departed for Madrid, via Copenhagen, on March 11. Upon arriving in Copenhagen, Doris and Trina Hosmer, Falcon Track Club teammate and training partner, asked if they could run from the airport to our downtown hotel. This was common practice for these two runners, and when they secured their baggage, they had my blessing to go. Thus began the almost daily ritual of the Brown-Hosmer run, with subsequent travel report—things to see, places to eat, things to do, etc. Those of us who did not run or were busy doing other things learned a great deal from those who did.

We arrived in San Sebastian eight days before the race. The city, a famous seaside resort, was essentially closed for the winter. Our accommodations were in an older hotel offering Spartan facilities and low-cost meals. We trained daily on the wide beach in front of the hotel, as well as on segments of the International racecourse. The weather, pleasant on our arrival, turned particularly nasty by race day, with rain and sleet pelting participants and spectators alike.

In spite of the weather, several thousand spectators lined accessible sections of the 3000-meter course, with hundreds more in the stands surrounding the "Hipodromo de Lasarte" where the race would start and finish. Our strategy on race day was for Doris to follow, not lead in the early, flat portion of the course then move decisively on a hilly, narrow trail where she had the best opportunity to run away from the competition.

"Veteran British runner, Rita Ridley took the lead as the race began and held it for the first 700m right into the face of a very strong and cold wind. At this point England's Angela Lovell, just 18, took over and tried to break away from the pack while the wind was at her back . . . Holland's Boxen-Lenferink and after a moment's hesitation Ridley, Brown and Christine Haskett also took out after Lovell."[31] Order of the lead pack remained the same as the runners departed the Hippodrome, disappearing like ghosts into swirls of sleet.

I have watched Doris run a hundred times, or more and two races that stand out as monumental were her world record mile in Vancouver on February 19, 1966, and her victory at San Sebastian. The racecourse outside the Hippodrome was a quagmire. Runners slipped and slid up hill, entered the woods, and were gone. Spectators stood silently in the cold—suddenly two runners re-appeared, Boxen-Lenferinik and Brown fighting for the lead.

Both runners saw it, an obstacle intended as a jump, dry yesterday, a torrent today. Boxen-Lenferink seemed to hesitate; Doris charged ahead leaping to the other side. She opened a lead and ran on through mud and mist to win her fifth consecutive international title. Doris' time was 11:08.4, Boxen-Lenferink was second in 11:21.2, and Trina Hosmer was 33rd. Trina, who just four weeks earlier had competed in the World Cross-Country Ski Championships in Sweden, commented after the race that the weather was right for a Nodric skier. She then said, "I needed my skis today."

Through out my coaching career, I have made an effort to combine travel with competition. In 1971, we traveled by train to Madrid, later flew to Seville, and then by auto to the Costa del Sol, on to Granada to view the magnificent Alhambra, back inland to Seville and home. The team loved it, especially the opportunity to run in the hills and on beaches near Malaga.

A funny thing happened in Madrid. Doris and Trina returned from a run one afternoon to inform me they had discovered a place where we could see Spanish dancers and had made a reservation for adult members of the team for that night. Later, upon arriving at the site of their discovery, we were to learn, this was an expensive restaurant with a cover charge for dinner and the show. At the women's insistence, we paid the cover charge, enjoyed the least-expensive dinner and prepared to watch the show. The dancers arrived. They were magnificent. We were enthralled, until at a break in the action when the MC came to our table and asked us to leave. The reason—Doris and Trina had fallen asleep and the dancers refused to go on with the program with women snoring in the front row.

Back in Seattle, Doris began to transition from cross-country to track in preparation for the Pan American Trials scheduled for April 30-May 1. The shorter 800m race made the transition all the more difficult. In her first race, a local event (April 5) Doris ran 2:10.2 for 880y. Two weeks later Doris placed 3rd at Mt. Sac, running 880y in 2:09.7. We did not panic, but rather decided to change tactics in the Pan Am trials hoping that would be a way to qualify for the Pan Am Team.

Doris, a front runner, usually set the tempo of a race, her competition content to follow. At Quantico, Doris stayed in the middle of the pack in her preliminary heat and her competition held back as well. When she made her move, it was too late for most runners to respond. She and Cis Schafer cruised to the tape together in identical times of 2:12.7.

"The final of the 800 meters was the most fiercely contested race of the meet. Crawford sped the field past the quarter in 61 then Brown huffed and puffed and stormed into the lead. Francie Johnson, who hadn't yet this year broken 60 in two consecutive 440y attempts, heard the lap time and hit the brakes as Gibbons and Schafer moved up. Fifteen yards clear of the field, Brown and Crawford moved the pace hard to the 660y pole then relented as Johnson and Schafer finally shook the determined Gibbons and started closing the gap. Down the backstretch, Brown applied the pressure and pulled away to best Crawford by a stride, 2:05.5 to 2:05.8, excellent early season time."[32]

I believe it is important to recognize that Doris achieved

the excellent early season time while doing primarily aerobic training. Recognizing that every person is unique, what I choose to call an experiment of one, it is my strong belief that most females who chose to compete in middle distance events will benefit from significant amounts of over distance, aerobic training.

The summer of '71 had only begun when Francie Larrieu and Francie Johnson made an all-out assault on the women's world record for the mile. Competing in Berkley on June 5, both runners were timed in 3:31.0 (68–2:20–3:31.0) through the three-quarter mark, with Francie Larrieu winning in record time, 4:41.5. Meanwhile, Doris who ran 2:07.4 for 880y in Seattle, on May 30, broke Francies' record by running a mile in 4:41.3 on June 6.

Six days later (June 12), while competing in the Rose Festival Track and Field Meet in Portland, Oregon, Doris lowered her world mile mark to 4:39.6. In an article appearing in the Portland Oregonian Doris is quoted as saying following her world record run "I train one day, limp the next and spend a third in traction."[33] It was only June; Doris was hurting. Yet one week after setting a world record. Doris had to prove her fitness by running in a so-called Pan Am show meet at Urbana, Illinois.

This was exactly the sort of demagoguery that controlled and crippled women in track and field for many years. Why hold the Pan Trials at the beginning of May if the games were not to be held until the end of July, with the USA-USSR dual and the National AAU Championships squeezed in between?

Why indeed? What sense is there in forcing an athlete to run for show when one week earlier she set a world record for the mile? This could only happen in the United States, and only with the then-prevailing system of qualifying for international competition.

To make a bad situation even worse, Doris was asked

to run 1500m on her arrival Urbana, not the 800m for which she qualified for the Pan American Games. The reason—the US needed additional strength at that distance in the forthcoming USA-USSR dual. As was her nature, Doris complied, winning the 1500m in 4:18.8.

As long as I can remember, goal setting has been an integral part of my life. My father was a goal setter, periodically using an aging spirometer to measure his lung capacity and that of all the neighborhood kids. He challenged me to set goals for chin-ups, push-ups, for my batting average, and for how far I could put the shot. When first working with Doris, I encouraged her to set goals. As we matured in our coach-athlete relationship, we shared in setting goals, achievable, yet at the edge of possibility. It was time to review and revise our goals for the summer that lay ahead: the USA-USSR dual July 2–3, National Track and Field Championships July 10–11, and the Pan American Games July 31-August 2.

After careful consideration, we decided to continue doing what had gotten Doris to where she was: train the "strong side," aerobic fitness, and mental toughness with particular emphasis on the 1500m/mile. The goal was competitive excellence on both sides, i.e. the faster 800m, the less fast 3000m and 2 mile. We had positive expectation that "strong side" training would, if the opportunity occurred, produce world record times in the longer events.

A Strange Thing Happened
on the Way to Berkley

With limited time to train before flying to Berkley, we chose to run repeat 220ys on the track and miles at red line (perceived as hard) off the track to prepare for the USA-USSR dual meet. Our goal was a 4:15.0 1500m. The final workout called for 20 x 220y x 30–32 sec. with a 110y jog back. The day was hot and dry, the workout intense. Rounding the curve on the 15th repeat, Doris went down as if she had been shot. I was at the opposite end of the field and began running to where she lay. Before I got there, a car slid to a stop. A man jumped out and ran to where Doris was twisting in pain. Seeing me, he asked "Are you responsible for this?" The man then acted as if he were going to strike me, at which point I helped Doris to her feet; both legs contorted with muscle cramps.

Dear, dear Doris, wet with perspiration, dirt streaked, obviously in great pain, turned to the man and said, "Please don't be angry . . . I am a runner. God gave me my body and I honor Him when I train as hard as I can."

Shaking his head, the man returned to his car and drove slowly down the street.

When Doris arrived in Berkley, US team coach Fred Moore, a longtime friend, asked her to run both the 800m and 1500m against athletes who he described as "extremely fit." On July 2, 1971, Doris and Kathy Gibbons faced their Russian counterparts in a race considered to be a kickers challenge. Doris led from the start in an attempt to take the kick out of her Russian opponents. As the runners rounded the final turn, Tanara Pangelova moved into the lead to win in the excellent time of 4:13.8. Doris was 2nd, setting a new American record for 1500m with the time of 4:14.6. She had achieved her goal of running a 4:15.0 1500m, but she did not win.

Coaches are frequently asked if so and so won his/her race—did his/her best—achieved a certain goal—was a winner. In pondering these questions, I have concluded that winning and doing one's best is not necessarily the same thing. Some wins come too easily, thus coming in first place in the contest, but certainly not a win where high achievement is concerned. On this day, in this race, Doris placed second—in doing so she did her best—in the best sense of the term her performance was outstanding—she was a winner.

On July 3, the day following her record-breaking

1500m, Doris and Terry Crawford "working together executed their race plan to perfection with Terry opening up the inside with 330y to go. Doris shot through into the lead and Terry fought Niola Sabaite as long as she could, but the Russian closed the gap in the stretch and won despite Brown's best time of the year."[34] Doris was 2nd again with a time of 2:04.7. She flew back to Seattle that evening to rest then prepare for the National Track and Field Championships, less than a week away.

In the summer of 1971, women had only been competing nationally/internationally in distances as long as 880y/800m for 11 years. The first such race, other than the scandal ridden ½-mile race at the 1928 Olympics, was conducted at Rome in 1960. Doris, as reported earlier, was third in the 1960 Olympic Trials and had continued to run 880y/800m as a primary track and field event. Even so, it was becoming abundantly clear that the 800m would soon be a long sprinters event and runners like Doris who lacked sprint speed needed to move up to longer distances to maximize their natural abilities.

The first officially sanctioned two-mile event was contested as a final on July 10, 1971. A new event in the Championship schedule, the two-mile attracted a huge number of entries. Included among the entries were the best of the cross-country runners in America: i.e. Vicki Foltz, Beth Bonner, Pam Bagian, and Cheryl Bridges. Doris led from the start as others seemed content to let her methodically grind out the laps. She covered the first mile in 5:10.3 and the second in 4:56.7 for a record time of 10:07.0. Falcon Track Club teammate Vicki Foltz was 2nd with a time of 10:34.1.

Returning to Seattle, Doris had two weeks to rest and train before leaving for Cali, Columbia, site of the Pan American games. My recollections and notes depicting what happened during those two weeks is indicative of my frustration at the system and my great respect for Doris. How could anyone, I wrote, cope with the psycho-physical burden of stepping up to the starting line in so many diverse and demanding competitions? Most of the great runners with whom I was acquainted could get up for one or two races, though no one other than Doris, to my knowledge, was able to compete at the highest level, over a period of months at distances from 880y to 2.5 miles, on the track and on a cross-country course.

During our many conversations I once asked Doris if she had any regrets about her running career. In the back of my mind, I had assumed that she might want to talk about the injuries that had impacted her training and performance, but this was not so. What she said surprised me at first, but after we chatted for a while, it all made sense. She said, "Not being able to do what I believed to be best was most harmful, especially the situation surrounding the Pan American Games—a qualifying meet three months prior to competing in Cali—the required show meet in which I was forced to run a mile when I would be running 800m in the Pan Am Games and then having to do what team coaches told me to do."

Doris was unique in her ability to compete with the best in the 880y/800m. She had modest foot speed but great aerobic power. She was a front runner who took the kick out of the kickers. Coaches for international teams on which she competed frequently instructed her to lay back until the final turn and then kick for home, a logical tactic for a runner with foot speed, a receipt for failure for a runner like Doris.

In Cali, Columbia, the 800m was contested over two days (July 31-August 1). Doris easily won her semi-final heat in 2:10.2. Teri Crawford won the 2nd semi-final heat in 2:10.7, with the Canadian champion Dr. Abigail Hoffman running just fast enough to quality. Doris and I were well aware of Hoffman's ability, as she and Doris had run against each other numerous times. Hoffman was a kicker. In order to beat her, Doris had to run Hoffman into the ground. That was our strategy when Doris departed for the Pan American Games. Brooks Johnson, Pan Am team coach, had other plans, instructing Doris to follow then kick off the final turn. Ever careful to do what she was told to do by an international team coach Doris followed and was beaten by Hoffman in 2:05.5. Doris 2nd in 2:05.9.

"I both regret and resent what happened to me in Cali." Doris said to me on her return to Seattle. Now fast forward to the Pan American Games of 1975. I was a coach of the US Team and director of our high-elevation camp at Los Alamos. One of the athletes with whom I worked at Los Alamos was Kathy Weston a 400m-800m specialist. Kathy had good foot speed and would likely run against Hoffman in Mexico, City. From day one, Kathy prepared for Hoffman's kick by engaging in a timing drill. A marker was placed at a point on the turn of our training track 150m from the finish line—the point at which Abby usually initiated her kick. For two weeks, Kathy listened for my whistle, a signal for her to jog to the marker prepared to kick a 150m in 20 seconds.

The result of the 800m in Mexico City is a highlight in my long coaching career. Not only did the race go as expected, with Hoffman kicking off the final turn, but Kathy was alert and ready, out kicking the defending Pan American Champion to win the gold.

Several months later, I received a letter from Kathy Weston, thanking me for working with her at Los Alamos and for helping her win in Mexico City. Kathy wrote, "The race was the most satisfying race of my life . . . I was at peace on the starting line . . . when she (Hoffman) started to kick I was ready, almost laughing all the way to the finish line."

Returning to Seattle from Columbia, Doris, too, was ready . . . for some rest. We did not train again until after Labor Day when school was in session and a routine returned to our lives. My records show little change in our normal fall routine: daily morning runs, weekend hikes, running, running, running over wooded trails, long stretches of parkway beside Lake Washington, the Arboretum, and a place known as "neckers knob," with its 300 stair steps in a one-mile loop.

The first real challenge in the fall of 1971 was the National AAU Championship cross-country meet. In addition to Doris, our Falcon Track Club had a full team for this national event. Doris won, the Falcon ladies were 2nd. When asked following her victory how many times she had won this event, Doris said, "I really don't know how many times I have won it" This was her 4th straight win, over a soggy course, 70 yards ahead of 2nd place Beth Bonner (14:29.0–14:49.0). Standing at the finish line to congratulate teammates and friends . . . shivering when asked about her victory, Doris' only response was "My feet are really cold."

I was there; that is what the champion said!

In a strange sort of irony, the night after the championship we could only afford to pay for two rooms at the YMCA in downtown Chicago. The rooms were cold and dirty. I shared the bedding from my single bed with the six members of our team in the adjoining room. In a typical act of humility and camaraderie, Doris volunteered to sleep propped against the wall in the shower. Doris was and is a true champion in every definition of the term.

PEAKS AND VALLEYS

1972 was the twelfth year during which Doris would engage in competition at the national level. Beginning with the 1960 Olympic Trials, her odyssey as a runner was similar to that of most persons who aspired to be the best, a long-term competitive experience marked with peaks and valleys, the very high, the oh so low. Like the limbs of the willow tree riding high on springtime breezes—low against the ground with winters cold.

Doris ran her first competitive race of the year in New York's Madison Square Garden (February 25) winning the indoor mile in 4:44.0. This was her third victory at the NAAU Indoor Championship event. Though her time was unimpressive, we returned to Seattle confident she was ready for what we considered a greater challenge, qualifying for her 6th International Cross-Country race.

In 1972, the national body recognized the importance of the international championship event, revising the qualifying procedure accordingly (as most cross-country coaches had advocated for years.) Rather than use the US National Championship to qualify team members, a special qualifying meet was scheduled for the first weekend in March, approximately three weeks prior to the international race. The first such meet was co-sponsored by the Seattle Department of Parks and Recreation and the Falcon Track Club. Sanctioned by the PNAC, the meet brought together 23 or the top 25 runners in the 1971 National Championship, plus three of the top five finishers in 14–17 championship and selected runners from Canada.

When meet entries lined up for the start, I thought to

myself, *These young ladies are likely the most select group of American and Canadian runners ever assembled for a cross-country race.* The 2000, mostly partisan spectators who lined the course seemed to agree, responding with overwhelming support—especially for their hometown heroin, Doris Brown. She did not let them down. Leading from the start, Doris seemed to glide over the 2.5-mile course. I can see her still, coming over the crest of a hill, a lone figure, so small, so timid, yet with a warrior's heart she came on to win—her time 13:27. A rising star, Eileen Clagus, was second in 13:31. The next five finishers were Tina Anex, Caroline Walker, Debbie Roth, Beth Bonner, and Jane Hill.

Later that evening, a post-meet banquet was held to honor all of the participants in the qualifying meet. When Jack Griffin, US Team coach, stood to congratulate the six runners who would accompany him to Cambridge, England, for the March 18 event, we were unaware of the shocking mandate to be received the following day. The mandate from the national office (AAU) was that Doris was obligated to compete in an indoor meet against the USSR rather than the International Cross-Country Championships.

To say that we were shocked would be a gross understatement, a world champion, team leader, running for her country and the possibility of winning a 6th international event, forced to participate in a meet for which she had not prepared. Sports writers in our city could not let this injustice go.

John Owen referred to the boondoggle as the "Gray-Green World of Doris Brown . . . a pack without a leader" is what he later wrote, and then he softened the pain somewhat, noting "In the world of Doris Brown there's always another race. There's this one, the last one, and the one yet to come." [35]

Dick Rockne wrote more critically of leaders in the AAU. In a front-page article appearing in the Sunday Edition, he quoted Doris' response to the mandate that she run relays when she should be defending her international record: "It's just incredible that the AAU would agree to a meet like that (with 600m-800m-1500m and 4 x 800m events) at a time when the top middle distance runners were hoping to run in Cambridge, England. Rockne also quoted me as I vented my frustration, saying, "I am very bitter." [36]

Little did anyone know how deeply I hurt for Doris, how very bitter I had become. Our spirits, like the limbs of the willow tree in spring, so high Saturday afternoon, were low, so very low by Sunday noon.

Years have passed since that day in 1972 when Doris glided over the rolling hills of Green Lake Park to win a place on the US cross-country team. I still do not understand why our governing body put pressure on her to run indoors, rather than defend her championship record. What I do understand with clarity is that one can be a champion in many ways. Though her spirit was nearly broken, Doris never let others know how deeply she had been hurt. She was hostess to members of the US team who stayed in Seattle to train, helping them with housing, taking them to her favorite places to run, arranging for meals, even assisting with the acquisition of the teams' travel outfits.

The final "stressor" (her words) for Doris in the "boondoggle" (John Owens' words), was having to request a change in the time and date for the oral defense of her masters thesis. The change was cause for Doris to spend a long night in Chicago's O' Hare airport in route to the Richmond meet. Upon arriving, she was told she would run the mile and a leg on the US 4 x 800m-relay team. She was 3rd in the mile (4:40) behind Russia's Pangelova (4:38.9) and Debbie Heald's world record of 4:38.5. She later ran 2:09.2 for 800m fastest for a member of the US relay team.

Dr. Harmon Brown, a longtime friend and a US team coach sent me a note several days after the indoor meet in which he said, "Doris looked tired . . . stressed, like her heart was somewhere else." His was a discerning view. Doris ran for her country, rather than for herself. When I saw her next, she was a different person. She had lost something difficult to define—like an edge gone dull. She was never quite as sharp again.

For several days after returning to Seattle, Doris did little other than work with a physical therapist to calm hamstrings inflamed by repeated tight turns on the indoor track. Her rehab program was designed for a progressive return to full activity: extensive stretching, hydrotherapy, walking then jogging and running. Progress was slow. Time had taken a toll on rehabilitative resources. Doris was no longer able to come back as quickly and completely as she had in earlier years.

It was nearly three months before Doris could compete again. On June 4, 1972, she ran her first race of the outdoor season posting a time of 4:17.4 for 1500m (68.4–2:19–3:29.4–4:17.4). We were cautiously optimistic. However, the following day Doris had difficulty running giving us cause to schedule a meeting with the entire rehab team. It was decided that Doris would by-pass the NAAU track and field championship, giving her additional time to prepare for the Olympic Trials. The decision proved to be prudent as Doris qualified for the 1972 Olympic team placing 3rd in the 1500m with a time of 4:18.4 (64.5–2:11.7–3:24.4–4:18.4).

Good news—Doris was pain free following the qualifying meet. She trained with renewed passion, running some of the best workouts of her competitive life. When she left for Munich, I flew to Europe as a tourist/spectator—a situation soon to change as Doris received permission form Nell Jackson, team coach, for me to work with her each day on the training track. I was with Doris the morning of her trial heat, leaving in time to watch her run.

Inside the stadium, expectations were electric as heats

and the names of contestants were posted on the main scoreboard. How proud I was to see the name "Doris Brown" in bright lights.

When contestants appeared, one was missing. "Where is Doris I called out?" For a moment, I stared in disbelief, then with tears burning my eyes I ran up the stadium stairs, across the highway, into the athletes' village, on to the warm-up track. Doris was nowhere to be found.

It would be hours before I learned what happened after I left the warm-up track that fateful day. Doris decided to run one last turn and stepped on a high jump cross bar extending onto the track. Trainers carried her to the infirmary where physicians put her foot in a cast; she was informed she "had broken her foot."

Much has been said and written about that stressful day in Munich three decades ago, but perhaps no one caught the essence of Doris' story more clearly than John Owen in his "Daily Olympic Report" Owen wrote, "The Olympic story is Lynn Colella wearing a silver medal on the victory stand, and trying to keep from crying. But it's also Doris Brown listening in stunned belief as the race she has been preparing herself for mentally and physically for months and even years finally gets underway without her . . . she still couldn't believe she was out of the Olympics before her first race, that countless hours of training and the moments of complete exhaustion were all now focused on this one point of pain."[37]

The games were over for us, and in less than 24 hours, the world would come to understand the ugly face of hatred as murders gunned down innocent Israeli athletes—our trauma, trivial, when compared with the loss of the Israeli team.

Returning to Seattle, Doris went directly to "The Sports Medicine Clinic" to see our team physician. Following a through examination, her injury was diagnosed as a ruptured peroneal tendon. Her prognosis was grim. It would be weeks before she would be able enter into a comprehensive training program—longer before she would be ready for competition.

It was ten weeks, to be exact, before Doris ran seriously again. Her first and final race of 1972 was the National Cross-Country Championships, held on a rolling, grass course in Long Beach, California. Doris ran with a determined courage, placing second behind the new champion, Francie Larrieu, San Jose Cinder gal. Doris had won every cross-country race she had entered in more than 12 years, except two: a loss in 1967 to teammate Vicki Foltz while rehabbing a torn hamstring and today.

In her special way, Doris congratulated Francie then stood for photos with her team—The Falcon Track Club. A headline in "Women's Track and Field World" summarized the event . . ."LARRIEU & FALCONS XC CHAMPIONS" . . . the writer then wrote "The Falcons, under the able direction of Ken Foreman, have been the tough luck team of distance running for many, many years, always turning up at Nationals with one or more of their fine stable of runners sick, injured, attending weddings or funerals. This time they were not to be denied as they poured it on the rest of the nation with Brown in second spot, Kathy McIntyre third, former National Champion Vicki Foltz fifth, Beth Bonner 9th and Laurel Miller tenth for a total of 29 points to 75 for runner-up San Jose."[38]

Doris continued to run competitively—though less frequently for several more years. Her big event in 1973 was the International Cross-Country meet held in Waregem, Belgium. Doris placed 15th Francie Larrieu 16th with Falcon TC runners Vicki Foltz and Kathy McIntyre well behind.

In 1974, Doris led a group of Seattle Pacific University students on a trek from Katmandu to the base camp at Mt. Everest. This was the closest she ever got to fulfilling a childhood dream to be the first woman to summit that awesome peak. On the long hike out, Doris fell and broke an arm. Two days after returning to Seattle, Doris ran with her team, The Falcon Track Club for the last time—placing 2nd to a teammate—rising star Debbie Quatier. The race was vintage Doris Brown—running with one arm in a cast, the other pumping like mad she completed the 3-mile course in 17:19.8.

An era was coming to an end—historically significant because Doris and her contemporaries were pioneers in the truest sense of the term. They were initiators, leading the way so thousands of girls and women might share in the joy of competitive running. Francie Larrieu, a pioneer, too, would emerge as a bridge between the old and the new.

Doris and Rita Lincoln, Great Britain, run stride for stride, Barry, Wales, March 18, 1967

Fatigued victor, Chino Milini Invitational, Milan, Italy, 1972

San Sebastian, Spain, Brown and Boxen-Lenferink fight for the lead, March 20, 1971

The shoe man said, "No one of any significance will ever come from this (cinder) track."

NAAU Championship One Mile Run, Madison Square Garden, February 23, 1968

World record for 1500m. The Seatle Indoor, February 7, 1970

Doris and Abbie Hoffman sprint to finish, Pan American Games, Cali, Columbia, August 1, 1971

Bell lap pre-Olympic 800m finals, Mexico City, October 15, 1967

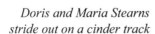

Doris and Maria Stearns stride out on a cinder track

Start International Cross-Country Race, Fredrick, Maryland, March 22, 1970

Doris ran twice a day for 40 years,
saying, "Runners just love to run."

Ken Foreman

FOOTSTEPS

I n the summer of 1973, the World University Games were held in Moscow. I was head coach for the US Team and chose to work with throwers and middle-distance runners. One of the athletes for whom I was responsible was Francie Larrieu. Francie came to that meet with clearly delineated training schedules, developed by her longtime coach, Augie Argabrite. My role in her final preparation should have been routine timing splits and facilitating travel to and from Lenin Stadium, but it proved to be far from ordinary. Two of the other than ordinary happenings related here represent significant insights into the subtleties of coaching and athletic performance. Both are keys to understanding the athletic genius of runners like Doris Brown and Francie Larrieu.

During the week prior to opening ceremonies, the US team trained in Lenin Stadium. On one of those days, I was timing Francie as she worked through a moderately difficult interval session—pace segments with jogging recovery. Focused on Francie, I was unaware that we had attracted a group of spectators, one of whom spoke to me during a longer period of recovery. The man asked in broken English, "Vat iss your runner doing?" Handing him my clipboard, I continued timing Francie. When the training session ended, the same man spoke again, saying, "Ve are all coaches . . . ve have studied you Americans for years. I see by your schedule that you continue to train to train, while we now train to compete."

Wow, was he on to something, or was that his way of telling me "Our system is better than yours." I tucked the comment into the corner of my mind and called down to

Francie, saying, "We need to hurry if we intend to catch the bus."

We missed the bus, had no way to call for transportation, so we decided to try our luck with the subway. While crossing a busy thoroughfare, we were stopped by a car in which there were four men. The driver called to us and asked, "Do you have money to change?" We ignored him and attempted to walk away—a second man asked if we "wanted to buy art treasures?" There were other questions, all which we had been instructed by state department representatives to ignore. Finally, the car and its occupants drove away. As we continued walking toward the subway station, Francie said, "I am uncomfortable here, constantly listening for footsteps."

We managed to find the correct subway and were on our way toward Lenin Heights when I asked Francie to tell me more about footsteps. She responded saying, "Being here in Moscow is something like racing, I am constantly aware of footsteps." Francie then said, "The most disconcerting thing about being where I am as a runner is listening to the footsteps of those who are attempting to catch me." Pausing, Francie said, "Now I know what it was like for Doris all of those years, those terrible footsteps following behind." Wow, another comment to stretch the mind!

I returned from Moscow never wanting to go back!

With the passing of time, I have come to recognize the importance of the Moscow experience for the questions raised—training to train and footsteps. How does anyone cope with the insidious nature of footsteps? How did a timid little girl who ran across tide flats on Puget Sound learn to deal with the thunder of the thousands of footsteps that she must have heard?

While pondering this question, I had occasion to talk with Doris about doubts or fears that may have hindered her performance. She was quick to say that downtime, waiting between heats for a race to begin, was most destructive to her. She then explained how difficult it was for her to leave a life situation filled with activity, to enter into a period of unreality where she did not need to think or plan or work, where everything was planned out for her. "The Olympics was the worst," she said, "because there was so much empty time. I was not ready for that."

Ed Temple, Dave Rodda, and I were sitting in the stands during a final heat in an international meet. An American hurdler, who placed 4th, ran back along the track to call out to her parents, "You don't know how badly I wanted third."

Ed turned to Dave and me and speaking from a lifetime of world-class experience he said, "This thing that we are doing either drives one up, or it drives one down. I heard that young lady talking on the team bus the other day, and she was bragging about taking first. Something happened to her when it came time to compete."

"Like hearing footsteps, I asked?"

Ed was quiet for a moment then said, "Perhaps. The sad thing is there isn't time enough for coaches to do much about it. When athletes come to us they either have it or they don't."

Some months later while addressing the team prior to the World Track and Field Championship in Helsinki (1983). I related an insight discovered in Howard Thurman's book *The Luminous Darkness.* Dr. Thurman postulates a theory about fear and courage in which one person's fear contributes to another person's courage. To paraphrase Thurman: There is a thing at loose in the world called fear . . . when I am filled with fear you are filled with courage . . . when I begin to get a little courage, you begin to get a little fear. . . and when I am filled with courage, you become filled with fear.

At the end of summer 1983, long after the World Championships ended, I received a letter from an athlete who stated, "I have always had problems at the end of my race, somehow letting runners of less ability beat me in the final kick. I have though a great deal about that fear thing and begun to assert myself coming off the final turn . . . the latter part of this season has been the best racing of my life."

Pamela Spencer was the first high school girl in America to high jump 6'. After graduating from high school in Great Falls Montana, she matriculated at Seattle Pacific University. I was her coach for two years. Pam qualified for the 1976 Olympic Team and was expected to be among the top performers in the Montreal event. On the day of her competition she jumped only 5'7"—well below a height she could jump almost anytime, any day. Pam did not qualify for finals in the 1976 Olympic Games.

Later, through tears, Pam said to me "I heard two voices out there today. One voice said, 'Pam, you are the best high jumper in the world. You are going to win the gold medal today.' The other voice, told me I was a loser. I would not jump well today. The tragedy," she said, "is that I listened to the second voice—and I am a loser."

In 1980, members of the US Olympic team were competing in a meet in the city of Cologne. As I recall, Pamela Spencer jumped 6'5" that night. What I do remember for certain is that she came to me after the meet to tell me she still heard two voices when she was on the field of competition. "The good news," she said, "is that I am listening to the voice that says I can, not the voice that says I can't."

I do not profess to have the answer, but do know the great ones are a different breed of cat. They hear footsteps, and they deal with them. They hear what I call "night sounds"—those ruminations with which we must deal in down times, those empty spaces so debilitating where peak-performance is concerned, and they cope. One reason Francie Larrieu and Doris Brown were champions is that they had the ability to deal with the awful sound of footsteps.

STEAM THAT DRIVES THE HUMAN MACHINE

I have struggled to fashion a title deemed appropriate for this final chapter—perhaps the most important chapter in this book. The reason for my struggle is I desperately wanted to get it right:

WHY did Doris run?

HOW was it possible for her to ascend from the Tide Flats of Puget Sound to the top of the athletic world?

Speaking metaphorically, WHAT was the steam that drove her machine?

When I first queried Doris about her motives for running, more specifically what the forces were that kept her going for more than a decade, which drove her to work hard enough and long enough to be champion of the world, she seemed perplexed, almost as if the answers were self-evident. Then after a long moment, she said, "I am certain of one thing, and that is, if you are going to succeed as a distance runner you have to love to run!"

Several weeks later Doris sent me a note saying, "I have given your question about running considerable thought, and here is a summary of my thinking."

(1) "It may be running away from something." Later she wrote, "Can't be too much of it . . . maybe a catalyst. Ken you helped me focus on how to run toward all the good and away from all the ugly."

(2) "The joy of running."

(3) "The tension of achievement . . . the goal . . . way to become more of who one is."

(4) "Something to give back." When I asked Doris if she wanted to amplify any of her comments, she said, "Just this . . . we are all different in the way we go about things, but I am convinced that it takes long, hard, tough training to be a successful distance runner!"

Having pondered the questions raised above for the better part of three decades, I share my best guesses as to how and why Doris came to be a world class middle distance, distance runner. The first, the easiest to quantify, are factors that can be measured on the track and in the lab. I discuss some of these in the opening section of this chapter. The nonquantifiable, existential factors, far more difficult to discern, will be discussed at the end of the chapter.

A significant part of my professional life has been focused on the elite athlete. Early in my teaching-coaching career, I became interested in the quantifiable factors related to the selection and training of high achievers in the athletic arena. For many years, I taught a graduate course titled "What We Know About the Elite Athlete." My students and I searched the literature to discover what was known and written about high achievers a search revealing, among other things, information regarding relationships between body morphology, size and form and successful achievement in selected athletic activities.

While on a fact-finding tour for USA Track and Field I met with West German sport scientists to learn more about body types and performance, as well as their national program for "talent identification."[39] The German national test protocol is administered to all students in primary and secondary schools, with specific focus on speed, quickness, strength, power, flexibility, and coordination. Young men and women are provided varying levels of assistance and subsidy, predicated on test scores.

Using the West German test as a model, I developed a field test battery for identifying track and field talent among

American school kids.[40] Analysis of data representing several thousand American school kids, tested with my field test, reveals a strong correlation between field test scores and performance potential. The question here is, would such tests have identified Doris as a potential world record holder when she first started to run? My answer is perhaps. My reluctance to say yes or no stems from the fact that we can measure objective things, but we cannot measure such factors as courage, commitment, and the strength of the human will.

The Quantifiable

There are, of course, many more quantifiable factors than those dealing with body type. I turn now to specifics where Doris was concerned. I personally measured her percentage of body fat, vital capacity, aerobic capacity, anaerobic power, strengths, flexibility, speed, and quickness many times. She was among a select group of female athletes tested in Humco 11, the advanced human body counter at the Atomic Energy Laboratory, Los Alamos, NM. Using both hydrostatic measures and measures accrued at Los Alamos, Doris' percentage of body fat ranged from 5.5%-8% during the years 1965–1972.

Several sport scientists other than myself tested Doris to determine her aerobic capacity. Scores accrued from these tests varied with the season, with the range of oxygen uptake scores 64–70 ml/kg/min. During peak training and competition, Doris weighed 107–110 pounds. Her record reveals best speed and speed-endurance marks of 25.3/200m and 55.3/400m. While not necessarily predictive factors, Doris could easily perform 20 pull-ups, climb a 25' ropes without using feet and legs and do 100 pushups.

The best of these marks for predicting performance potential in middle distance, distance events are oxygen uptake and times for the 200m-400m. With uptake marks of 64–70, Doris would be considered an outstanding candidate for middle distance-distance races. (This is particularly true for the 5K-10K and marathon, which are distance races added to the women's schedule long after Doris ended her competitive running career.)

Doris' foot speed, however, would be seen as a limiting factor for the 800m. Madeline Manning and Charollete Cook, her toughest competitors in the late '60s, were both significantly faster than Doris, both having 400m speed potential of 51–53 seconds.

On the basis of quantifiable field test scores, it can be stated that Doris had a checkered field test score card— great aerobic capacity, excellent body morphology (size and weight), significant physical strength, but limited speed. It is safe to say that during most of her career, Doris was competing in races too short for her natural gifts, which again raises the question, "How did she do it?"

When one looks at body density measures and upper body strength, Doris appears to be a superstar. We know body density has a strong correlation with middle distance/ distance performance, and it is my best guess that upper body strength does as well. Strong arm action and relaxed shoulder girdle muscles are keys to a successful final kick.

Over a period of years, I tested rowers from the University of Washington Crew to determine aerobic capacity and accrue related findings from maximum work on a motor driven treadmill. After one test session, I met with Dick Erickson (deceased), crew coach to discuss the physiological implications of test results. Dick listened attentively for several minutes then said, "Ken, I am not really interested in that stuff. The reason I am having you do this is so I can look into the eyes of my guys when they think they can't take another step and see how they respond."

Wow! My focus as an exercise physiologist was on objective data. Erickson's focus as a highly successful veteran coach was on more subtitle, though equally important subjective things. Both are important when working with and/or attempting to understand what makes an individual perform.

There are in the athletic domain many platitudes, some of which are perceived as fact. One of these is the oft quoted cliché "No Pain-No Gain." While I do not accept this as fact and have ended training sessions when seeing pain in Doris' eyes, her comment to a friend gave me cause to ponder. I overheard this comment: "Pain is my friend, reminding me that I am working as hard as I am able to work." When Doris put her twist on the subject, pain took on a wholly different dimension—a nonquantifiable dimension. The focus in the remainder of this chapter is on nonquantifiable, existential-personal things that likely contributed to Doris' success as a runner.

The Nonquantifiable

In a very real sense, looking for clues as to why some naturally gifted individuals become high achievers and others do not is like attempting to define a subjective phenomena like love. We can see what is accomplished in the name of love, care, concern for others, sacrifice of self for a larger cause, obvious things. Yet it is not clear what love is. In the same sense, we can see what Doris accomplished while not being able to specifically say how or why, even though we try. And try we must for the sake of those who aspire to achieve and struggle toward some higher place.

Perhaps the most frequent response to the question why: Why do you train so hard, why do you persist at doing what you are doing, why, why, why?

"I enjoy travel, meeting people, experiencing new and challenging situations." Doris often reminded me of a little girl who set out to see the world, and in many ways, she was. She also was a person who had done her homework;

she knew a great deal about the places we were to see. I first learned this when we visited the village of Eaton following her victory at Barry, Wales. Doris seemed to know all about the village and the school where so many of England's most influential leaders had spent their formative years.

When Doris qualified for the team trip to San Sebastian, Spain, she immediately obtained a copy of Michener's Iberia. Having read the book, she was our cultural guide in a country rich with tradition and intrigue. Her enthusiasm for looking and learning was contagious, even for those who seemed to be content to sit in the hotel, play cards, and talk.

Though not directly related to the question of why Doris trained, a true travel story may offer other insights into the nature of Doris Brown. We were walking back to our hotel after a long day of sight seeing in Paris when Doris suggested that we rent a car and travel to the coast. She then surprised me saying, "I would like to visit Flanders Fields."

"And how," I asked, "do you know about Flanders Fields?"

Her response left me in stunned silence as she recited a poem learned in elementary school.

> In Flanders Fields the poppies blow
> Between the crosses row on row
> That mark our place; and in the sky
> The larks, still bravely singing, fly
> Scarce heard amid the guns below.
> We are the Dead. Short days ago
> We lived, felt dawn, saw sunset glow,
> Loved and were loved, and now we lie
> In Flanders fields . . . . . . [41]

The trip to Flanders Fields was a turning point in our relationship as athlete and coach. We had just enough money to rent the smallest of cars, purchase a large block of cheese, several loaves of bread, and we were off on our odyssey.

That first night we ate cheese and bread and slept in our little car. In the morning, both of us were in need of bathroom facilities, but none were to be found. Even now, Europe is not famous for its public facilities. In 1967, they seemed to be nonexistent. Our first hope for relief was a mom-and-pop gas station. Doris started to open the door of what appeared to be a rest room, and the wrath of heaven came down on her. We were not certain why such a response. We just shrugged and agreed that certainly did not work.

We continued to drive, looking for a tree or a haystack, any place where we could relieve our building pressure. Finally, we saw a small train station and slid to a stop. "Ladies first," I said through clenched teeth. Doris ran into the little station. There was loud talking in French, and then silence. Assuming all was well, I entered the little station just in time to see Doris in a squatting position. To my dismay, she made a well-known sound. I looked up and an elderly French railroad man had a smile on his face. Now he understood, the lady was asking if she could use his bathroom.

The bathroom was two foot prints and a hole in the floor, but what sweet relief because of creative action by the newly crowned champion of the world.

During the years that she was competing, nearly everyone who watched this quiet, self-effacing woman run asked, "How can she turn into such a terror on the track or the cross country trail?"

Ben Mitchell wrote after interviewing Doris and watching her run: "It's her dedication, determination, and endurance to run that last, lonely mile in training."[42]

Ask Doris' running partners and they would have agreed; she had unbelievable determination. Some would argue that her determination had no limits. It saw her through pain and injuries and endless hours of grueling road work. It is what put her in the Olympics and earned her countless titles and awards.

Kimball Bender has written about "the music of her spirit." "Whenever I see Doris", she said, "I am struck by the feeling that she is physically present with her body, but that her mind is always churning about something. She is intense in her love for God and the gift she feels she was given to run. Her mission in life has been to be ever mindful of how she is using her gifts. It isn't about winning or going to races, it's about how you get there and how you continue along the way . . . Her passion to run goes deep and her resulting work ethic is extraordinary."[43]

Bart Wright, writing retrospectively quoted Doris in his search for motive and dogged pursuit of excellence. "Doris" he wrote, "believes that it may be too easy for females today . . . it's amazing that while athletes have better opportunities now, it doesn't seem to have helped them use their potential . . . in days when things were really tough, you had to want it so badly, your mind had to be so much into it, you really gave yourself to it in a way athletes today don't understand."[44]

Listening to Doris chat with a journalist one day I caught a far more subtle, though perhaps more profoundly important, factor in her willingness to work and struggle and hurt and persist. It was the word "friendship." I must tread carefully here, as it would be easy to overstate the truth, but much has been written about the power of friendship. For example, it is said that during times of danger and difficulty, friends willingly sacrifice everything for a friend. I asked her about this one day as she waited for her afternoon running group to assemble. Doris was quiet for a time then said, "If you are asking about my motives for running, I know that setting goals has been important to me, but far more important are the friendships that have made the endless work worthwhile."[45]

She then talked quietly about people you meet and people with whom you work as "friends of a kind," noting

Ken Foreman

"They might be friends simply because you are with them all of the time. That is not like friends I have in track . . . persons with whom I have shared about as severe stresses and challenge as two people can." She sat quietly, then said, "It is like you are on the starting line at the Olympics: you're all by yourself, but these other people are there experiencing it too. Suddenly you realize you know something about each other that can't be shared by most people in the world. It's a common bond that gives you a feeling that is sort of above and beyond everything else."

Doris and I were socializing with a local family following her victory in Barry, Wales, and the man of the house, a sports photographer, asked, "Why did you start running?" The man, a Gordon Roberts, also a cross-country buff, was like most "Brits," unaware that American women were running, let alone competing in distance events.

I will never forget that evening because we also met two delightful, though tipsy, English women who 30 years earlier had been professional sprinters, running for tea cups and cooking pots. They knew why they started running. "It was a way to earn prize money—other prizes too." Nevertheless, they, like Gordon, wondered why one would run when they had to pay their own way?

That night was the only time in our long association that I heard Doris say, "When I started to run, I discovered a new kind of joy, perhaps the first real joy that I could remember. I forgot the problems and pressures at home and then I ran for the love of it." [46]

Research focusing on why girls choose to participate in athletic activities reveals that the two most frequently noted reasons are parental support and sibling modeling. Doris had neither. Her father all but forbade her from joining a track club, her mother was neutral, and her brother and sister were not athletic.

Over the years, especially the later years when things

did not always go the way we expected, I queried Doris about her motives for continuing to train and compete. "What," I asked, "is the steam that runs your machine?" Invariably, she said, "I love to run . . . Most of us who run well love to run." As an afterthought, she said, "The more you invest, the tougher it is to give it up." Even now at age 62, she reminds me that with all her anomalies, if she has a choice, she will run, noting "It is a lifestyle; I can do nothing less."

How many times have I watched as Doris and her teammates—Vicki Foltz, Trina Hosmer, Laurel Miller, and Debbie Quatier—run off as if in a flight of joy. I hear them talking, laughing, and singing their way through a park or on a wooded trail. Invariably, they return wet with sweat, hair wild and tangled, carrying flowers in their hands.

On those occasions when I could not or did not accompany Doris as she traveled to national-international competitions, we communicated almost daily by telephone or mail. Her messages manifested a sense of reality, yet they also carried the song of joy and hope. During a particularly long and tedious trip, she wrote "Half the team has been sick, In Augsburg lots of athletes couldn't run. I tried to remember back to what I did before successful runs . . . I was off the track for over a week . . . beaches and roads, enjoying the country. So Vicki and I did park running . . . beautiful, streams, natural woods, paths and a river . . . I was anxious for the Augsburg race."[47]

During the toughest of days on her first visit to Los Alamos, when we were learning and Doris was paying the price, she wrote, "I'd hate to feel much more exhausted." Later she wrote, "Morning runs have been great . . . we have found logging roads, paths down canyons and up mountains. The wild flowers and fragrant evergreens are delightful. Sometimes we are gone several hours." Workouts did not get much easier, but after discovering canyons and mountains, wild flowers and evergreens, Doris' spirit was lifted, she could write, "I'm thinking with singleness of purpose . . . feel better about doing it . . . the hard work of preparing for the Olympic trials."[48]

Some years ago, I was asked to organize a summit for distance runners to be conducted at the Squaw Valley Olympic Training Center. During the opening session, participants were told to "sleep in" the following morning. "Rest up from your travel," I said. When we coaches went to the dining hall the next morning, none of the runners appeared. Odd, but after all they had been advised to "sleep in." As Dr Harmon Brown and I left the dining hall, he pointed toward a mountain peak, saying, "That is a great place to ski."

Then we saw them. Tiny specs high above the valley, our women, up and running while we were asleep. I remembered what Doris always said to me, "Runners love to run." *Yes,* I thought while standing with Harmon, *what we are seeing is who you are. This is what you do; this is an existential thing.*

In my hierarchy of values, work ethic or what I perceive to be a "principled effort" to get a job done ranks near the top. Indeed, I frequently tell my student-athletes that the highest recommendation that I can give them is that they have a positive work ethic. Packing a 20# watermelon to the top of Mt. Rainier likely is an indicator that one has a positive work ethic.

Mt Rainier located in Washington State is one of the tallest peaks in America (14,410'). Encircled by glaciers, it can be a formidable challenge to even the best of mountaineers. Over the years, a number of climbers have fallen to their death, including five in 2004. Doris' Odyssey on this great mountain was a test of sorts, the final challenge for students who were preparing to trek from the city of Katmandu to the base camp at Mt. Everest. *Wouldn't it be nice,* she thought, *if I could surprise those who reach the summit with a slice of cool, fresh watermelon?* (The melon was frozen solid when they reached the summit.)

Most climbers who struggle up the more than 6000' of rock and steep, fractured ice and snow carry only what they need for substance and safety: ice axe, crampons, down clothing, gloves, wind gear, other emergency things. However, Doris is not like most climbers/people; she also carried a 20# watermelon to share with her students and friends. When I talked with her recently about carrying a watermelon to the top of Mt. Rainier she replied, "It wasn't hard for me to do at the time," reminding me of all those years when she trained so hard that she could scarcely speak. I realize even more so now that Doris' work ethic was an asset of inestimable value in her rise to world stature as a runner.

When talking with or listening to high achievers in the physical domain, they often speak about the "feeling." It felt so good; when asked to explain, they use terms like balance, harmony, rhythm, and beauty to explain what they mean. In an interview with Diana Montgomery Doris talked about feeling in saying, "I get a feeling of freedom from running . . . Green Lake so often is beautiful. It is a place to think, a way to keep life in perspective. And it is relaxing, not exhausting. It helps me be more disciplined in the rest of my life."[49]

More recently, Doris expressed a similar sense of feeling when she said "I think the aesthetics are what I love most about running. For me it was the feeling of being at one with nature. I hate to call it endorphins, but there is a feeling when you put yourself out there a little bit on the edge of your comfort zone (that) this is important."[50]

Years ago while backpacking in the Sierra Nevada Mountains I met a man who was running the length (20–30 mile each day) of the Pacific Coast Trail from Mexico to Canada. When asked about the difficulty of his venture, why he chose to do such a thing, this hot, dirty, and sweat-drenched man quickly replied, "I love running, especially in evening when the sun is setting—when I sense the rhythm of the universe."

Doris knows about such rhythm, once saying to me, "There is rhythm to my running . . . a joyous, happy rhythm beneath my feet."

Adding another twist to this theme Steve Kelley wrote, "For Heritage running is as natural as breathing . . . the beating of her feet has kept her alive as much as the beating of her heart."[51]

Why is any of this important? Does it matter why a person chooses to run?

It matters on a personal-existential level. It matters, too, when beginners begin to run. A wise, old coach once said to me, "The secret, Ken, is keeping the scoffers long enough to pray."

I have learned that most high school kids start running for reasons having little lasting power, affiliation, a kind of herd warmth. There seldom are brass bands or cheerleaders where runners trod. It often is hot or cold or wet or too lonely to carry on. For those who come for affiliation or for those who are running away from something or for the uncommitted, the journey is soon over. There is not sufficient steam to run their machines, but for those with a purpose, there seems to be!

Remember the story about the motorist who stopped to aid Doris who had fallen to the track in pain? He stopped by the track several days later to watch and to learn. When he left, he said, "I have always wondered how it is that some people seem to catch a vision for their lives, and then have the guts to hang in there until their vision becomes a reality. I think I see it now. It is Knowing where they are going, a purpose that keeps them focused on their goal." Then, as if an afterthought, he said, "Thank your girl for me. She has taught me an important lesson for my own life."

There is a lesson here for all who seek some higher place. The lesson is that we all are different. We likely are motivated by different things: travel, love for our sport, a positive sense of self-worth, a challenge, sense of rhythm, or feeling good in the zone. Yet the surest source of steam to run our machine is purpose, a clear sense that I know where I am going and a vision of how best to get there. All of her life, Doris has had a fundamental belief in the goodness of people, in a God in whose image she was created, and in meaning and purpose bigger than herself. Such a clear sense of meaning and purpose, coupled with unique physical gifts and mental toughness, surely was and is the source of her success. Steam enough to carry a kid with a dream from the tide flats of Puget Sound to the higher places of the world.

Ken Foreman

Epilogue

While the primary focus of this story is an accounting of circumstances that shaped the life of a teenage girl, nudging her to follow her dreams in a sometimes disinterested and even hostile environment, to become one of the premier middle distances runners in the world, her life obviously did not end with the NAAU Cross-Country Championships of 1972. Indeed, by virtue of her 2nd place finish at Long Beach, Doris joined the US team at the International Cross- Country Meet in Waregem, Belgium (March 19/73), where she was the top US finisher.

On April 14, 1974, Doris proved her competitive fitness by winning a 1.5 mile Green Lake Dash in 7:35 (mile split 5:06). By virtue of her time, she was invited to run 5k in the prestigious "Restoration Meet" in Eugene, Oregon (February 8/74). On February 22, 1975, Doris posted a time of 13:00.3 in a 2.5-mile race on her home course at Green Lake in Seattle. Although now fully engaged in teaching and coaching, she continued to serve as team leader of the Falcon Track Club, a role in which she nurtured many potential national caliber runners, including Debbie Quatier and 13-year-old record setter, Deanna Coleman. On November 7, 1976 pupil and mentor ran 1st and 2nd in the dual meet of the decade between the FTC and the San Jose Cindergals. Doris' time for 2.7 miles was a respectable 15:28. One week later, she placed 5th in the NAAU Championship meet at Miami, Florida.

In May of 1976, Doris ran her first marathon, finishing first among women in the Lions Gate Marathon in Vancouver, BC. Her time of 2:47:36 was the third fastest ever run by an American woman, set a Canadian record, and was posted as the 5th fastest in the world. It staggers the mind to contemplate what Doris might have accomplished in distances longer than 1500m had she been given the opportunity to compete in such events at her competitive prime. Even so, her accomplishments were appropriately recognized when (October of 1976) Doris was named "Washington's Woman of the Year."

In her last race of note, Doris won the National Masters Cross-Country championship at Raleigh, NC in November of 1988. While her competitive running career was waning, her involvement in the activity she loved so dearly was enhanced in other ways. On May 3, 1973, Doris was named to the USOC Athletes Advisory group—the first of a progressively more prestigious list of appointments, which included the role of assistant coach for the 1984 US Olympic Team, the 1987 World Championships Team, team leader for the U.S. Ekiden cup contingent in Japan, and the USA entry in the USA-Great Britain Cross-Country dual meet in 1993. Perhaps her most noteworthy assignment was her election as the first woman to serve on the prestigious IAAF Cross-Country and Road Race Committee in 1988.

Doris has served on the coaching staff at Seattle Pacific University for nearly 40 years, 26 of those years as head coach of cross-country. She has been named "Conference Coach of the Year" six times. She has produced two Olympians (Bente Moe and Gitte Karlshoj), several National Team members, more than 50 All American athletes, as well 5 NCAA Champions and NCAA record holders.

At a more personal level, I am pleased to say (I was her Department Chairman) that Doris has been and continues to be an innovative and forward- thinking leader in higher education. When asked to teach a course in kayaking, she instituted a build your own boat program in which dozens of university students planned, designed, and constructed their kayaks. She instituted one of the first cross-country ski courses in the Pacific Northwest, leading hundreds of students into the back country of the Cascade Mountains.

Perhaps her most noteworthy innovation was the implementation of a unique study-travel quarter. In 1974, Doris planned, organized, and implemented the so-called "Nepal Quarter," in which she and nine students hiked from Katmandu to Kalipatar, high on the flanks of Mt. Everest. Class work included study of the Sherpa language and a project in the students major. Doris notes with pride that all of her students did advanced level degree projects, very high quality and beneficial to everyone on the trip. She continued, saying that "Contacts with schools, hospitals, police, etc. made the trip very educational." Indeed, one of her students was so deeply impacted by the Nepal experience that he has since committed his life to working with disadvantaged peoples in the far corners of the world.

The Heritage that Doris now proudly claims as her married name eventuated as a consequence of the Nepal Quarter. The short version goes something like this. One of her students was having difficulty carrying her pack up and down a particularly torturous segment of trail, so Doris offered to lighten the students' load, which of course added to the load that Doris was carrying. While assisting the student over a precipitous place, Doris fell and broke her arm. A man whom she had met but did not know came to the rescue of both the student and the instructor. He helped guide the student to a Sherpa hut, later locating a doctor who could cast Doris' broken arm. For the remainder of the journey, Doris and Ralph Heritage were trekking partners.

When discussing this portion of her life journey, Doris notes, "When we stepped off the airplane in Seattle, we said our good-byes and did not see each other again for several months." Over time, however, mutual friends nudged us back together. We were engaged, and set a date to be married at Green Lake, where I had run hundreds, perhaps thousands of miles." It was a simple service with a reception befitting a world champion runner with most of the attendees participating in the inaugural Doris and Ralph Heritage Green Lake Biathlon.

The Last Mile

I had finished writing and was working on the Appendix when one of my oldest friends called to ask, "Why weren't you there today?" This is no ordinary friend; he was a shipmate in the South Pacific, a track nut, a high school vaulter who was at one time a teammate of Coach Dean Cromwell's "Valorous Vaulters" Earle Meadows and Bill Sefton.[52] My old shipmate is quick to say that the peak of his track and field career was jumping against the greatest of the great on a bamboo pole, the late Dutch Warmerdam. "Yet today," he said, "was an experience I would not have wanted to miss."

It would be difficult to explain to an 86-year-old friend, world famous mountaineer, veteran of K2, fellow in the American Alpine Society why I did not travel to Seattle to watch Doris run her last mile, when he did. Rather than attempt to explain, I asked my friend, Dee Molenaar, what it was like to be there. "You missed a great event," he answered. "Hundreds of people joined Doris on the track as she ran her last competitive mile." Adding, "Most of us had tears in our eyes."

Dee was, of course, referring to an event organized to honor a great champion and to give friends and former athletes the opportunity to celebrate a life committed to excellence by joining her on the track one last time. Doris, who was scheduled for hip replacement surgery, would never run again. Steve Kelley described the scene this way "Some 200 friends-former teammates, former students and people who just wanted to say they had run with Doris Heritage joined her for those final four laps.

As Heritage angled around the turn and accelerated into the final kick of her career, her friends kicked with her and cheered as she blissfully glided the last 100 meters . . . It was one of those small, throat-clenching moments that remind you how great sports can be when all of the veneer is stripped away, when no owner of television or pampered super star is around to spoil things.

It was a moment as pure as Oxygen."[53]

That pretty well sums up the competitive life story of Doris Brown Heritage. It has passed as quickly as a kick to the finish . . . sometimes blissful, sometimes not, but ever "as pure as oxygen."

And I shake with joyous laughter when I think about it. Doris was up at 4:00 A.M. on the day of her surgery (June 1, 2004). She slipped on her singlet and shorts, pulled on her shoes as she had done for more than 45 years, petted her aging dog named Zola Budd, and was out the door for another run.

APPENDIX A

Training format, implemented in March 1965, daily morning run of 4-6 miles.

Monday   8 x 220y in 34-35 sec. with 220y jog back recovery. We increased volume adding 2 220ys/week for a total of 16—thereafter increasing intensity with the final goal 16 x 220y in 30-32 sec.

Tuesday   Speed day 10 x 100y fast stride—walk back recovery
We added 2 100ys/week for a total of 20 at 95% speed. Rest to work ratio always met or exceeded 10-1

Wednesday   Long intervals—660y-1000y. A typical work out would be 3 x 660y with a 10-minute jog interval or 2-3 times the length of the race for which one was preparing. (In her peak years, Doris ran 660y repeats in 1:32-1:35.)

Thursday   Usually an over distance day—a fun run or Buddy run away from the track—talking pace 45-60 minutes.

Friday   Ladders, power runs, diagonals—varied distance, intensity and volume

Saturday   Complete rest

Sunday   6-8 recovery run

Appendix B

IN THE LEGISLATURE
OF THE
STATE OF WASHINGTION

Whereas, Doris Brown, a resident of Seattle, Washington and a teacher at Frank B. Kellogg Junior High School in the Shoreline District, on Saturday March 18 1967, at Barry, Wales won the International cross-country race for women, defeating her nearest competition by more than 100 yards; and

Whereas, Doris Brown in 1966 won the national women's cross-country and 1,500 meter championships; and

Whereas, Doris Brown, by her diligent training and hard work, has set an honored example for her pupils, and has brought great credit to Kellogg Junior High School, and to the Shoreline School District, and to the State of Washington; and

Whereas, the members of the House of Representatives of the State of Washington desire to pay tribute to her and to express their gratitude for the honor which she as brought to this state;

NOW, THEREFORE BE IT RESOLVED by the House of Representatives of the State of Washington that this body hereby acclaims and honors this woman for her outstanding accomplishments and, more especially because she has chosen a career in our public schools where she can be a shining example of this state; and

BE IT FURTHER RESOLVED, that this body expresses its hope that Doris Brown may have the opportunity of successfully representing the United States of America at the Olympic Games in Mexico City in 1968; and

BE IT FURTHER RESOLVED that the Clerk of the House of Representatives shall suitably inscribe copies of this Resolution and furnish them to Doris Brown, to the student body of Kellogg Junior High School, and to the Board of Directors of Shoreline School District.[54]

Appendix C

Training at Los Alamos
September 5-14, 1968

All participants in the high elevation camp trained twice daily. Three mornings each week, track athletes ran easy aerobic miles at an elevation of 8500', on alternate days they ran 30–40 minutes on the Los Alamos Country Club golf course. Afternoon training sessions occurred on the Los Alamos High School track. Following is a ten day training cycle for selected members of the 1968 Olympic Team.

September 5

Doris Brown, Nancy Shafer, Francie Kraker

5 x 150y fast strides—150y jog back

3 laps of jogging recovery

5 x 150y fast strides—150y jog back

10 minutes of jogging on grass

10 x 75y sprints—75y walk back

Madeline Manning not feeling well walked for 30 minutes

September 6

Brown-Shafer-Kraker

3 x 100y-220y-330y—100y-220y-330y jog back—splits 13.5–28.0–42

10 min easy jogging

1 x 330y-220y-100y—330y-220y-100y jog back—splits 43–28–13

With 6 hours rest Doris ran a 4:52.4 mile in an exhibition event for local track and field fans. (69.0–2:18–3:37–4:52.5)

Manning walked 30 minutes

September 7

Brown-Kraker-Lois Drinkwater

3 x 330y step down—100y walk back—splits 48–46–44

15 minutes easy jogging

10 x 100y finish simulators—100y walk back

September 8

Morning only—One hour fartlek at 8500'

September 9

Brown-Kraker, Manning, Shafer, Drinkwater

10 x 220y—150y jog back—all between 27.5–29.5

15 minutes of easy jogging

6 x 150y—150y jog back—all between 18.5–19.5

September 10

Brown-Shafer-Kraker-Manning

600y time trial

| Brown | 57.3–1:21.3 |
| Manning | 57.2–1:21.5 |

Kraker   57.5–1:22.0

Shafer   58.0–1:23.3

15 minutes of jogging

8 x 75y fast stride—75yd walk back

15 minutes of jogging

220y with running start—wind aided

Shafer 24.6 Brown 24.7 Kraker 25.5

Manning hurting did not run

September 11 Full day of rest—optional trip to Frijoles Canyon

September 12

Brown, Manning, Kraker

2 x 440y x 58—440y jog between 1–2

15 min jog

3 x 330y step down—220y shuffle interval—splits 49–45–41

September 12

Brown, Kraker and Manning

2 x 1000y—15-minute walk-jog recovery

Brown-Manning 2:33–2:36

Kraker 2:35–2:38

September 13

All middle distance runners—45 minute buddy run.

September 14

Brown, Kraker and Manning

220y pace—220y stride—220y pace—440y jog—9 total 220ys.

Target times 28–36–28

15 minutes of jogging

1 x 550y x 75 sec.—550y jog-150y finish simulator-1 mile Jog down

APPENDIX D

Selected Performance Marks 1960–1972

		1960	
July 16	880y	2:17.6	Olympic trials
August 19	440y	59.4	AAU
August 27	220y	28.0	AAU

		1961	
January 28	880y	2:29	Mid-Winter Games
June 3	880y	2:21.2	Far Western AAU

Doris sustained stress fractures in both feet, did very little competitive running.

		1962	
May 4	880y	2:17.1	Vancouver, BC
July 7	880y	2:17.9	PNAAU

		1963	
May 4	880y	2:21.8	PNAAU
May 24	880y	2:18.9	Vancouver Relays
June 1	880y	2:17.1	BC Open (record)

1964

June 20	880y	2:21.5	PNAAU
July 25/26	880y	2:15.1	NAAU Hanford, Ca
November 28	2000m/cc	7:01	National AAU

1965

March 6	300m	41.8	BC Mid-Winter Games
	600m	1:42.9	
April 4	440Y	59.0	FTC Invitational
May 8	800m	2:17.1	Vancouver Relays
June 15	800m	2:14.1	BC Invitational
August 14	880y	2:16.3	Seattle Highland Games
	mile	5:21.6	

1966

February 19	mile	4:52 (4:33.3 1500)	World Indoor records
April 16	880y	2:09.7	Falcon Invitational
May	800m	2:14.9	Vancouver Relays record
May 13	880y	2:13.5	Angels Invitational
June 6	880y	2:11.1	PNAAU
	1500m	4:26.3	
July 2	1500m	4:20.2	NAAU
July 8	880y	2:08.5	Washington vs. W. Canada
	440y	56.7	
July 17	880y	2:05.1	Berkley, CA
September 9	Doris fell while teaching soccer and separated her shoulder		
October 8	3 mi/cc	17:14	Ran with arm in a sling
October 22	1.5 mi/cc	7:25.6	BC Championships
November 26	1.5 mi/cc	7:51.1	NAAU

1967

February 4	880y	2:08.5	World Indoor record
February 11	880y	2:09.6	Times Indoor Games
February 16	mile	4:40.4	World Indoor record
March 4	880y	2:09.2	NAAU Indoor
March 18	2.5 mi/cc	14:28	Barry, Wales
April 3	880y	2:10.9	PNAAU
July 2	880y	2:03.6	NAAU
July 8	880y	2:05.5	USA-British Commonwealth
August 15	800m	2:06.5	Pan American Trials
August 29	800m	2:02.9	Pan American Games
October 15	800m	2:09.6	Mexico City
November 22	3000m/cc	9:57	PNAAU

Ken Foreman

			1968	
February 4	mile	4:54.6		Seattle Indoor
February 17	mile	4:51.1		Achilles International
February 23	mile	4:50.2		NAAU Indoor
March 24	3000m/cc	15:00		Blackburn, England
May 28	mile	4:51.6		Oregon AAU
June 10	800m	2:05.7		Compton Invitational
June 11	mile	4:42.2		PNAAU
July 20	800m	2:02.2		London, England
July 24	800m	2:07		Dublin, Ireland
August 18	800m	2:05.1		NAAU
August 24	800m	2:03		Olympic Trials
October 20	800m	2:03.9		Mexico City
November 1	800m	2:05.6		Santiago, Chili
November 2	400m	56.2		
December 12	2.7 mi/cc	15:08.7		Green Lake, WA.

			1969	
February 16	800m	2:10.2		BC Indoor
March 22	4000m/cc	14:46		Clydebank, Scotland
May 3	800m	2:10.9		All Comer meet
June 3	800m	2:07.4		Compton-Coliseum Relays
July 6	1500m	4:27.3		NAAU
July 18	1500m	4:16.8		USA-USSR
September 28	1500m	4:19.9		Tokyo
	800m	2:05.4		
November 8	2 mi/cc	10:05		PNAAU
November 15	4000m/cc	14:28		Canadian Nationals

			1970	
January 31	mile	4:46.1		Portland Indoor
February 7	1500m	4:21.1		Seattle Indoor-World Indoor record
February 13	880y	2:09.5		Times Indoor Games
February 21	800m	2:07.3		Regina, Saskatchewan
March 22	2.5mi/cc	15:04.4		Fredrick, Maryland
April 25	880y	2:08		Mt. Sac Relays
April 26	3000m	9:44.6		World Record
May 17	mile	4:47		Vancouver Relays
	800m	2:12.1		
June 13	mile	4:45.2		Portland
	800m	2:06		
July 4	1500m	4:24.3		NAAU
November	2 mi/cc	10:50		PNAC
December 18	3 mi/cc	17:40		FTC Invitational

1971

January 19	800m	2:12.7	U. of W. Indoor
January 30	mile	4:45.6	Oregon Indoor
February 6	800m	2:07.3	Seattle Indoor
February 26	mile	4:47.3	NAAU Indoor
March 20	3100m/cc	11:08.4	San Sebastian, Spain
April 5	880y	2:10.2	All Comer
April 24	880y	2:09.7	Mt. Sac Relays
May 1	800m	2:05.5	Pan Am Trials
June 6	mile	4:41.3	Tacoma, WA-world recor
June 12	mile	4:39.6	Portland, OR-world recor
July 2	1500m	4:14.6	USA-USSR, American record
July 3	800m	2:04.7	
July 10	2 mile	10:07.0	NAAU
August 1	800m	2:05.9	Pan Am Games
October 9	2.5 mi/cc	13:44	Casey Invitational
Nov. 28	2.5 mi/cc	14:29	NAAU Championships

1972

February 25	mile	4:44.0	NAAU Indoor
March 4	2.5 mi/cc	13:27	Green Lake, Seattle
March 20	mile	4:40.1	USA-USSR Indoor
	800m (relay)	2:09.2	
July 10	1500m	4:18.5	Olympic Trials
September	Doris was injured while warming up—did not run in 72 Olympics		
Nov. 25	2.5mi/cc	13:34	NAAU

Reference List

Thurman, Howard. The Luminous Darkness. New York; Harper and Row, 1965

INDEX

FOOTNOTES

[1] http://www,jewishvirtuallibrary.org/Terrorism/munich.html

[2] Tacoma News Tribune, June 9, 1960

[3] Gateway, Thursday, June 23, 1960, No. 10

[4] Grant Kerr, Vancouver Sun, February 20, 1966

[5] Eric Whitehead, The Providence, February 20, 1966

[6] Harland Beery, Director, Seattle Pacific College News Bureau, April 17, 1966

[7] Dick Rockne, The Seattle Times, June 26, 1966

[8] Lorna Griffin, Letter to Author, Dated May 12, 2003

[9] Wilbur Ross, Personal communication during Pan American Games, Puerto Rico, 1979

[10] George S. Meyers, sports editor, The Seattle Times, Feb. 5, 1967

[11] Glenn White, staff writer, Orange Coast Daily Pilot, Feb. 10, 1967

[12] Mike Glover, P-I sports writer. Feb. 17, 1967

[13] Manchester Guardian, Manchester, England, March 20, 1967

[14] Ben Mitchell. Scanner and King County Labor News, Jan. 3, 1969

[15] George Meyers, sports editor, The Seattle Times, Feb. 6, 1967

[16] Los Angeles Times, June 4, 1967

[17] Wenatchee Daily World, Dec. 9, 1968

[18] Bob Payne, Spokesman Review, Feb. 4, 1968

[19] Mal Watman, Athletics Weekly, March 3, 1968

[20] Bill Schey, Bremerton Washington Sun, March 16, 1968

[21] John Owen, sports editor, The Seattle P-I, July 12, 1968

[22] Leo Davis, The Oregonian, Oct. 20, 1968

[23] John Owen, sports editor, The Seattle P-I, October 20, 1968

[24] Vince Reel, Woman's Track and Field World, December 1969, Vol. 3, N0.7

[25] George Meyers, The Seattle Times, Feb. 8, 1970

[26] Los Angeles Times, Feb. 14, 1970

[27] Women's Track and Field World, April 1970, Vol. 4, No. 4

[28] John W. Steward, sports writer, The Baltimore Sun, March 23

[29] Women's Track and Field World, January-February, Vol. 5, No. 1/2

[30] Olann Cassell. Letter to the author, February 18, 1971

[31] Women's Track and Field World, April 1971, Vol. 5, No. 4

[32] Women's Track and Field World, May 71, V01.5, N0.5

[33] Leo Davis, staff writer, Portland Oregonian, June 13, 1971

[34] Women's Track and Field World, September-October 1971, Vol. 5, No. 9

[35] John Owen, sports editor, The Seattle P-I, March 5, 1971

[36] Dick Rockne, sports writer. The Seattle Times, March 5, 1971

[37] John Owen, sports editor, The Seattle P-I. September 5, 1972

[38] Women's Track and Field World, November/December 1972, Vol. 6, No. 11/12

[39] Bernie Wagner, Stan Huntsman, Russ Rogers and Ken Foreman, 1979

[40] The Athletics Congress USA, Track and Field Coaching Manual, 1981

[41] "In Flanders Fields" was written by Lt. Colonel John McCray, MD on May 3, 1915 the day following the loss of a young friend and former student. According to some "In Flanders Fields" is one of the most memorable poems ever written

[42] Ben Mitchell, Scanner and King County Labor News, Jan. 3, 1969

[43] Kimball Bender, Northwest Runner, June 2002

[44] Brad Wright, "Doris Heritage: An American Pioneer," Bellevue American, May 8, 1976

[45] For insights into friendship in times of stress read "The Warriors-Reflections On Men In Battle," Chapter three. Love: War's Ally and Foe. University of Nebraska Press.

[46] From my personal notes written in a Barry Hotel the night after the first International Cross-Country race

[47] Letter from Doris dated August 10, 1969

[48] Letter from Doris dated June 3, 1968

[49] Seattle P-I, January 17, 1969

[50] Steve Kelly, The Seattle Times, May 16, 2004

[51] May 16, 2004

[52] Southern California Athletic Association

[53] Steve Kelley, times staff columnist. May 16, 2004

[54] Resolution No. 67–68 by Representatives Holman and Bluechel. Adopted by the House of Representatives April 4, 1967

Contact Ken Foreman
foremanken@hotmail.com

or order more copies of this book at

TATE PUBLISHING, LLC

127 East Trade Center Terrace
Mustang, OK 73064

888.361.9473

www.tatepublishing.com